"Kai Nilsen [is] a pastor with a vulnerable heart and a voice of experience and depth, calling and inviting us to join him in a journey toward wholeness in Christ. The path described in *Renew Your Life* is not distant or obscure. It is available and accessible, especially to those who are tired, worn out, beaten down or just lonely. Catch the energy that is described in this book and you might just find yourself renewed!"

Keith J. Matthews, Azusa Pacific Seminary

"Kai Nilsen is a fun person to have for a friend. It helps that he's a Lutheran. His first solo book project, *Renew Your Life: Discovering the Wellspring of God's Energy*, documents his own movement from running on empty to tapping into a source of vitality that is not of this world. Along the way he reminds us that the creation story was not a one-time-only event and fills this book with picturesque speech and practical suggestions. And it comes from a seasoned pastor's heart."

Gary W. Moon, executive director, Martin Institute and Dallas Willard Center, author of *Apprenticeship with Jesus*

"*Renew Your Life* is disarmingly honest, refreshingly faithful and profoundly hopeful. In a culture that increasingly confuses busyness with fulfillment, Kai's book is a roadmap, charting a realistic pathway to wholeness."

Jeff Marian, Prince of Peace Lutheran Church, Burnsville, Minnesota

"When the best wisdom that our age can muster is 'keep calm and carry on,' what happens when you hit a wall and there's nothing left to carry on with? In *Renew Your Life*, Kai Nilsen writes movingly about his own journey towards wholeness and lovingly points us to the substantial and constantly renewable reservoir of God's grace. For all who are weary, and any who have hit a wall, here is hope and life and healing."

James Catford, group chief executive of the British Bible Society (BFBS)

"How easy it is to lose our way, to say 'yes' too often, to allow our work to devour us, to get too tired, to overextend, to run out of gas in a misguided, self-absorbed quest to help God and other people. How can we find our way home to the rich wonders of God's grace, the possibilities that God sprinkles into every day, meaningful work, the beauty and mystery of nature, and the restorative rhythm of Sabbath rest? Kai Nilsen is a wise, insightful, empathetic guide for God's weary wanderers, gracefully helping us to reset our compass to the true north of the kingdom of God. Highly recommended."

Christopher Hall, Eastern University, and president of Renovaré USA

"With practically perfect timing for a digitally connected yet detached world, Kai Nilsen digs into the deep wells of biblical wisdom to bring to light the important challenge of rediscovering and reclaiming vitality and energy in life. It's a must read for busy people who are chasing, but not catching the wind!

Mike Housholder, Lutheran Church of Hope, West Des Moines, Iowa

"Kai's well-written book is a personal story about spiritual entropy. What happens when we run out of energy, or when we think we self sustain by our own power or ability? God brings renewal for Kai, and perhaps through his story, for you."

Peter Nycklemoe, senior pastor, Central Lutheran Church, Minneapolis, Minnesota

"Perhaps you are among the many who would say that they have become numb—numbed by unrelenting stress, numbed by the superficiality of relationships, numbed because of work that has become meaningless and empty, and even by the numbness that comes from compassion fatigue. Grace-filled and authentic to the core, Kai Nilsen has written a book that will wake you up, renew your life and energize you with fresh insights wrapped in the free gifts of God."

Rick Barger, president, Trinity Lutheran Seminary, Columbus, Ohio

"With compelling stories, delightful humor and rich prose, Kai Nilsen speaks a hopeful word to all who thirst for new vitality in life. By honestly sharing his own loss of energy, Nilsen invites readers, especially those looking for a way out of their own dispiritedness, into a grace-filled conversation about God's renewable energies. By dipping into the richness of the creation story, Nilsen suggests modest practices that have worked to energize his daily life. I discovered here a hopefulness rarely found in such books."

Ann M. Svennungsen, bishop, Minneapolis Area Synod, ELCA

"Changing one's life after years of patterns, habits and broken promises is one of the hardest things to accomplish. In his new book, *Renew Your Life*, my friend Kai Nilsen unlocks the secrets of creative energy as the source of the power needed to fully experience a new vision for life and a better understanding of how we are forever in the midst of a vibrant and vital life in spite of the cultural distortions that work against us. This book gave me a new energy for life."

Juanita Rasmus, pastor, St. John's Downtown, Houston, Texas

"Kai has written a great help. Many will find that this work gives way to a new beginning—a genesis of sorts. I certainly have."

Nathan Foster, Andrews Chair for Spiritual Formation, Spring Arbor University, author of *The Making of an Ordinary Saint*

renew your u r life

Discovering the wellspring
of God's energy

kai mark nilsen

Foreword by James Bryan Smith

IVP Books

An imprint of InterVarsity Press
Downers Grove, Illinois

InterVarsity Press
P.O. Box 1400,
Downers Grove, IL 60515-1426
ivpress.com
email@ivpress.com

InterVarsity Press® is the book-publishing division of InterVarsity Christian Fellowship/USA®, a movement of students and faculty active on campus at hundreds of universities, colleges and schools of nursing in the United States of America, and a member movement of the International Fellowship of Evangelical Students. For information about local and regional activities, visit intervarsity.org.

Scripture quotations, unless otherwise noted, are from the New Revised Standard Version of the Bible, copyright 1989 by the Division of Christian Education of the National Council of the Churches of Christ in the USA. Used by permission. All rights reserved.

While any stories in this book are true, some names and identifying information may have been changed to protect the privacy of individuals.

Cover design: Cindy Kiple
Interior design: Beth McGill
Images: Summer Days on the Coast by Paul Wadsworth/www.paulwadsworth.co.uk

ISBN 978-0-8308-4604-7 (print)
ISBN 978-0-8308-9879-4 (digital)

Printed in the United States of America ∞

green
press
INITIATIVE   As a member of the Green Press Initiative, InterVarsity Press is committed to protecting the environment and to the responsible use of natural resources. To learn more, visit greenpressinitiative.org.

Library of Congress Cataloging-in-Publication Data
Nilsen, Kai Mark, 1963-
  Renew your life : discovering the wellspring of God's energy / Kai Mark Nilsen.
    pages cm
  Includes bibliographical references.
  ISBN 978-0-8308-4604-7 (pbk. : alk. paper)
  1. Christian life. 2. Holy Spirit. 3. Spiritual life—Christianity. I. Title.
  BV4509.5.N55 2015
  248.4—dc23
                            2015022731

P	21	20	19	18	17	16	15	14	13	12	11	10	9	8	7	6	5	4	3	2	1
Y	33	32	31	30	29	28	27	26	25	24	23	22	21	20	19	18	17	16	15

To my mom and dad for giving me a vision of
a grace-filled world, and for living as if
your lives depended on it.

Contents

Contents

Then I considered all that my hands had done and the toil I had spent in doing it, and again, all was vanity and a chasing after wind, and there was nothing to be gained under the sun.

ECCLESIASTES 2:11

I will cause breath to enter you, and you shall live.

EZEKIEL 37:5

Foreword

James Bryan Smith

Wﾞhen I read Kai Nilsen's insightful and encouraging book, *Renew Your Life*, I kept thinking, "I know this story. I know these truths." But I could not recall where I had read them. About the time I finished the book it hit me. Kai was describing the classic Christian conflict described by the apostle Paul: "Walk not according to the flesh but according to the Spirit" (Rom 8:4).

I believe that in this fine book Kai Nilsen has given us a modern look at the same problem, the same struggle and the same choice that Paul was writing about. In place of the language of flesh and spirit, Kai invites us to consider modern equivalents—our spirits paralyzed by the weight of choice in a consumer world, longing to experience the freedom of simplicity in the world God desires; our minds numbed by demand and external expectation, craving a sense of God's delight in us and internal affirmation of God's love; our bodies wearied by the pace of life desperately seeking renewal by the ever present breath of life, the Spirit of God.

Kai is honest, even vulnerable, in this book. He will tell you that he—as a pastor—lost his passion for ministry, that he con-

templated leaving the ministry, that he battled discouragement
and disillusionment and nearly gave up. He confessed his
struggle to his father, hoping for a piece of wisdom or a word of
encouragement. He didn't get it. His father simply said, "You
may have to muddle through this for a while." While this advice
was honest and true, it was not what Kai wanted to hear.

But it was what he needed to hear because it led him on an
inner journey that only he could take. No one can take this journey
for us. Fortunately, in this book we get the benefit of journeying
with Kai and learning valuable truths that could serve as pre-
ventive medicine for many of us. Along this journey Kai encoun-
tered many people who helped him find his way, each offering
pieces of a larger puzzle. Some allowed him to explore his emp-
tiness and longing and gave him glimpses into their own understanding. Another would offer him a puzzle piece in the form of
a spiritual practice such as breath prayer. Another would offer him
a puzzle piece in the form of a word of grace: "You need to figure
out who you are, not what you think you should be."

This book chronicles Kai's attempts to restore the energy he
once had but had lost along the way, and energy he says he
"desperately needed in order to revitalize [his] work and refresh
[his] relationships." He narrates his story of energy depletion
and shares how he discovered the renewable energies of God,
the same mystery Paul describes when he writes about *walking
in the Spirit.* This book, Kai states, is intended "to give you tools
for tapping into the divine flow of creative energy." Gladly, he
succeeds. Kai is helping the modern reader understand what it
means to set the mind on the Spirit and to walk in the Spirit
and thus find life and peace . . . and energy.

We learn that when we walk in the Spirit we are accessing an
energy that is *renewable.* It never runs out. We learn that when

we walk in the Spirit we are accessing an energy that is graceful, possible, paradoxical, natural, relational, fruitful and restful. This energy is grace—it is not earned, but freely given to those who would surrender and receive it. It is full of possibility: there is no limit to what it can do. It is paradox: it is not black and white, simple and easy, but like life, requires that we hold opposites in tension. It is natural: the created world is charged with it. It is relational: it is accessed when we, with authenticity, seek to know and be known. It leads to fruitful labor: it energizes us to be creative and productive. It is restful: it revitalizes. Finally, we learn that renewing our lives with this renewable energy is not a quick process, but a slow one.

The book provides more than just a narrative of healing. It is filled with wonderful, probing questions and with helpful practices. The process of asking and answering questions provides a space for grace for the reader, a chance for the Spirit to reveal things to us we might not otherwise see. The exercises he suggests are challenging yet doable. They, too, allow the Spirit to enlighten and strengthen us along the way. In this sense, we are actually taking the journey with the author as he tells his story.

The energy depletion Kai experienced was the natural result of setting the mind on the flesh. Paul uses the word *flesh* (Greek *sarx*) when he describes such things as living with envy, trying to be religious, wanting to appear something we are not and striving for success according to values of this world. Someone jokingly said that they thought Kai should simply buy a little red sports car and get over it. But this would have played right into the hands of the flesh and made him more depleted, unhappy, dissatisfied and discouraged.

Instead, Kai chose the way of the Spirit. He began with an honest assessment of his condition. He admitted he was at the end of his rope, which is a wonderful place to be. Dallas Willard often remarked that "God's address is at the end of your rope." Kai sought God, and God was faithful. The world screams at us, "seek more and more," while offering us less and less. In this marvelous book, Kai gently reminds us that our souls demand not more and more but that which is more essential. May God bless you in the reading of this book and provide a wellspring of energy that enables you to do more than you could ever ask or imagine.

Introduction

Energy Depletion

His lips were moving, but I could barely hear a sound. Unfulfilled dreams, a meaningless job, a relationship devoid of energy—a different conversation, but the same old story circling round and round again. Though the narrative had not changed, something was dramatically different that day—not in him but in me. As we sipped our coffees and rummaged through his life once again, a startling thought passed through my mind: I did not care. I did not care about his life. I did not want to hear about his struggles. I was not interested in his relationships. I did not care.

I was shocked to admit that I, a pastor, could not fill the empty space between us with an ounce of compassion. Such compassion had always been a hallmark of my ministry. As the conversation dragged to a merciful close, I escaped to the solitude of my car, called my parish administrator and told her to cancel all my appointments for the rest of the day. Then I fled to the safe confines of my living room.

Slumping into the couch, I gazed through the picture window only to discover that even the vibrant hues of fall appeared bleak and gray. The same tree I had admired for ten years now mocked me. The same friendly neighborhood seemed devoid of life. I was dying from the inside out and could envision nothing life giving, nothing energizing, nothing vital happening in my life. Ever. Again.

How many of you identify with this story?

My story is my own, but I know it is not unique. In Western culture, too many of us are attempting to navigate the mind-numbing pressures of our lives with eyes blank, spirits diminished, relationships drained. Though we appear orderly and presentable on the outside, within our energy has drained away. Paradoxically, what we often need the most—the renewing energy of connective relationships—is what we have the least time and energy to pursue.

In 2013, the Barna research team highlighted a disturbing trend:

> Ten years ago, slightly over one out of 10 Americans self-identified as lonely. Today, that number has doubled—a paradoxical reality in the full swing of the social media age. . . . "As a nation, we are embracing the digital revolution and, ironically, we are becoming a lonelier population. While there are many benefits of being participants in possibly the most relationally connected age in human history, the social media revolution has not made us feel more connected, less lonely, or replete with friends."[1]

This book chronicles my attempts to restore the energy I once had, the energy I desperately needed in order to revitalize my work and refresh my relationships. I write hoping that readers struggling with similar issues will not feel alone, will find helpful guidance and will be renewed in their ability to access life-giving energy. As the apostle Paul reminds us in Colossians, "For this I toil and struggle with all the energy [ἐνέργειαν] that he powerfully inspires within me" (Col 1:29).

Jürgen Moltmann captures the concept of vital living in his book *The Spirit of Life*. "Here we shall interpret vitality as love of life. This love of life links human beings with all other living things, which are not merely alive but want to live. . . . Love for life says 'yes' to life in spite of its sicknesses, handicaps and infirmities, and opens the door to a 'life against death.'"[2] This vitality of life pulses through all of creation—from the ever-expanding universe to the vibrating subatomic particles at the core of all existence. It pulses through the dynamic forces of the natural world that transform the breathtaking beauty of autumn foliage into the bleak gray of winter and then into the lush green of spring. It pulses through the transforming cycle of human existence from life to death to life. The same God who breathes life into creation and into dead bones (Ezek 37) refreshes our bodies, restores our relationships and revives our energy for serving. This wellspring of life energy was present from the creation of the world and is presently available to you through God's Spirit. Perhaps you have experienced this energy for life in the dynamic movement from vibrant joy to numbing depression and back to vitality again. Or perhaps, like me, you are stuck somewhere between boredom and depression, and you fear you will never get out.

Sitting in a coffee shop working on my iPad, a software update notification appeared. Having the time and space available, I mindlessly clicked update, then moseyed over to purchase another cup of coffee. When I returned, the update was complete, and I was astounded to discover that Siri, the voice-activated software, was now live on my iPad. I asked myself, *How does that happen?* Moments before, no Siri. Now, this remarkable expanded capacity for communication. Nothing had changed in the physical structure of the tablet. The update was accessible whether I clicked on it or not. Simply by being open to receiving this update and intentionally saying yes, a new capacity for my work was unlocked.

Thrilled, I launched Siri and asked her, "Siri, what do you do?" She responded with lists of possibilities: make a phone call, check a contact, launch a web search, and on and on. In one moment, what I thought was impossible became possible.

In the same way, I am convinced it is possible to discover the wellspring of God's creative energy by intentionally and purposefully opening ourselves to it and letting it expand our capacity for more vital living. Creative energy empowers our lives, allows us to interact more energetically with others and connects us more intentionally with all of creation. This creative life change enables us to find the courage to

- say no to an addiction and yes to life
- gain new insight into how we are designed and linked to the web of creation
- forgive others and reconnect relationships
- participate in loving service with and for others

Over the past decade I have been fascinated by stories I have heard from friends and acquaintances about their creative life changes. Whether losing weight and recovering a new vitality in body, wrestling through a relationship issue and discovering a new vision for their common life, or overcoming a destructive habit and experiencing new freedom, the generative energy behind the change and the sustaining energy that led them through the change were described in similar ways. They adopted a new vision for their life, whether driven by fear or hope. They knew and were willing to embrace the struggle inherent in the process of change. They were strengthened and encouraged by some relationship. And they intentionally crafted a new rhythm of life that supported the desired behaviors.

The change themes were so consistent that I wondered about a common source. Then, it hit me. This wellspring of renewing life energy is articulated in the story of creation (Gen 1:1–2:4).

Embedded in the Creation Story

The biblical creation story is often considered a description of what God did in the past. However, Christian theologian Claus Westermann states that this creation story is not a static event but a dynamic, ongoing source of power and inspiration for each generation. He writes, "All over the world people know that their existence and their relationship to the world goes back to a beginning and they try to relate this beginning in some way to the present; . . . they trace back to its source the power which carries on their existence from generation to generation."[3]

Within the creation story, I have uncovered seven creative, renewable energies that were unleashed and continue to empower life from generation to generation. We do nothing to deserve or earn them. They come from God's loving and gracious hand. We are designed to receive and use them as a wind turbine is designed to pick up the energy of the wind and turn it into power. And these energies are renewable; they will never run out. The seven creative, renewable energies include:

Grace (Gen 1:1). Receiving the grace of life itself, I open myself to God's ever-flowing energy in which I "live and move and have [my] being" (Acts 17:28).

Possibility (Gen 1:2). Hovering over the waters of chaos, the Spirit of God makes possible hope for the new things God has already declared (Is 42:9).

Paradox (Gen 1:4). Wrestling with the reality of both light and darkness in our lives and in the created world, we receive the energy to move from suffering to endurance to new character to hope that will not disappoint us (Rom 5:3-4).

Natural world (Gen 1:9-25). Tapping into the ever-present wonder of God's creation, we learn what the natural world teaches us. "Consider the lilies of the field" (Mt 6:28).

Relationships (Gen 1:26-27). Opening ourselves to the divine image in the other, we discover the vitality that comes from relationships. "And who is my neighbor?" (Lk 10:29).

Fruitful work (Gen 1:28). Engaging our daily work we multiply our capacity to contribute to the good of the world. "For this I toil and struggle with all the energy that he powerfully inspires within me" (Col 1:29).

Rest (Gen 2:3). By embracing a sabbath rhythm for life, we learn to let go and trust God's providential care. "My presence will go with you, and I will give you rest" (Ex 33:14).

I call these *creative, renewable energies* for three reasons: First, they are *creative* because they are embedded in the creation story and, therefore, accessible to all. You do not have to consider yourself an artist to receive these creative energies. They are simply the energies we all need to live vibrant, vital lives. Second, they are *renewable*. Unlike a gas tank that runs dry or an oil field that becomes depleted, these energies are always available, waiting for us to access them. Third, I use the term *energies* because they infuse power for living and for loving service. For instance, the energy of grace connects us to the God who loves us no matter what, freeing us from the burden of others' expectations or our own harsh self-critique. God's grace is embedded in the creation story and renewable from generation to generation. The energy we gain by receiving this gracious presence makes us more alive and more willing to participate in loving service.

Each of these creative, renewable energies will be explored in subsequent chapters. But, before we proceed, we need to name and reflect on three particularly debilitating cultural distortions that can deplete us: (1) the pace of life, (2) our quick-fix mentality and (3) the seduction of more.

Pace of Life

"How are you doing today?" I asked my friend as we passed in the coffee shop. "Busy," he responded, and I nodded a *me too* nod, thus relieving each other of having to take time to talk.

"What's up?" I asked my teenaged son. "I'm busy, Dad," he responded. I nodded a *that's good* nod and left him alone.

"Time to talk?" a staff member texted. "Busy right now," I texted back. "Important?" "Not really," she responded. She understood—maybe.

In its recent research, the Barna Group points out a subtle shift in our common language. "It has been noted that the new default answer to the standard, 'How are you?' is no longer, 'Good,' but, 'Busy.' Such busyness is often perceived as 'the new normal' of the 21st century."[4] The effects of this busyness are many and varied:

Less quality time with children
Less time making love
Less time eating meals together
Less time talking to friends and family
More time glued to our smartphones
More fast food on the fly
More time in front of a screen
More frustrating time in cars

All of this has produced a culture filled with physically exhausted, emotionally enervated and spiritually empty people. Is it any wonder that we so seldom feel the joy of vitality, the power of energy? What makes this issue so complex is that we recognize the seductive power of busyness in our lives, have experienced its detrimental effects, but we cannot imagine an alternate way.

Quick-Fix Mentality

"Seven Quick Steps to Serenity," the announcement proclaimed. All I needed to do was come to a lecture, buy a book and follow those quick steps, and I would be there. I would have it. Seven seemed doable, the steps were orderly, and best of all, it was quick. I could fix myself and then get to work on all those harried, stressed, overworked people around me. Get them fixed. Quick.

The quick-fix mentality of consumer culture has perhaps produced marginally effective results in the short term. However, for the development of a deep life in the Spirit, the quick-fix mentality is counterproductive. Millions of books that promise simple answers to complex life issues have been sold, consumed and discarded, and yet our lives are increasingly lonely and enervated. Consumers have overdosed on quick fixes, but they haven't produced lasting personal change or necessary social change.

In my personal circumstances, what I failed to understand was that in my attempt to get past my pain and do it quickly, I was confusing technical problems with adaptive problems. Technical problems ask the question, How? and are problems of logistics for which we already have the necessary know-how. In my case, a technical problem was, how could I schedule my life in such a way that I could balance my spiritual and emotional needs with all the demands of home and career? Solution: I could open up my calendar and attempt to make time for each.

Adaptive problems ask the question, Why? and challenge values, deeply held beliefs and behaviors, according to Heifitz in *Leadership Without Easy Answers*.[5] Again, in my case, I needed to ask such questions as, Could I be a good parent and not be at every event? What would my kids think of me? What would other parents think of me? Will my kids succeed if they are not pushed in academics or involved in sports or music from the earliest age? Can I be an effective pastor without being present for every meeting? Is it possible to choose a life that does not require two full incomes? And why are all of these questions so important to me?

These are my questions at my current stage of life. What are yours right now? Do they require technical solutions or adaptive life changes?

In the face of these questions and through my reading and observing, I now realize that movement toward a more vital life can happen over time, as the daily habits we have created are examined and reshaped, as our habits of mind are questioned and recast, as our hearts are molded and stretched. The problem is in the phrase "over time." Letting anything emerge gradually over months and years is difficult. But such is the nature of creative life change.

The Seduction of More

My wireless carrier recently launched a "More Everything" plan. I can get more data, more talk, more text, more international calling, more, more, more. Even though I know the game, even though I understand they just want me to pay more money over more time, even though I am very satisfied with my current plan, every time I see the commercial a part of me wonders what it would be like to have more.

I am a living example of the pernicious soul twisting of Western culture—the seduction of more. Nothing is ever enough. We think a new car will make us happy, and maybe it does for a brief moment, but then we see our friend driving a bigger, better car. We think a new home will make our lives easier, our relationships more loving, but soon find that it is the same old same old. We think that losing a few pounds, building stronger muscles and tighter abs will give us delight in our bodies, but looking in the mirror tells us it is not enough. We are not enough.

When have you noticed this in your life? What form does it take?

The seduction of more also affects my understanding of my life with God. I think I should be more like ____ who prays an hour a day, or more like ____ who loves to study Scripture, or more like ____ who spends hours a week serving the homeless, or more like ____ leading the charge on environmental issues. In our minds, living more with more always trumps living more with less.

These three distortions—pace of life, a quick-fix mentality and the seduction of more—are impossible to avoid in our culture. The best we can do is tap into the wellspring of God's renewable energy to daily, hourly, thought by thought realign our thinking. The intent of this book is to give you tools for tapping into the divine flow of creative energy. You will be invited to read, reflect and talk with others, gaining wisdom from the written word, insights from your own mental and spiritual reflection, and the informed support of trusted friends to help you in this lifelong process.

To that end, throughout the book you will be invited to pause and reflect on a number of questions. I am convinced that the process of asking and reflecting on good questions is of greater benefit to a maturing faith and a more energized life than seeking simple answers. My hope is that you will not simply devour the words on the page like a fast-food burger but chew the concepts slowly and carefully, savoring the sacred nourishment that comes from deliberate, conscious reflection.

Beginning in chapter two when we explore the seven energies, you will notice what I call "Essential Life Questions." Creation narratives across cultures were written down and told in response to the essential life questions, "Where did we come from?" and "Why are we here?" These questions connect us with the core of who we are: our relationship with God, ourselves, others and the world.

The Essential Life Questions in chapters two through eight will invite you to probe deeper into each of the identified energies of God. To use an earlier concept, they are adaptive questions because they press us to question our core beliefs, values and habituated patterns of living.

If you are anything like me, I quickly scan questions I read thinking I will get back to them later but then rarely do. If that is you, let me make a suggestion: focus on the Essential Life Questions. Some of the questions you will have ready responses to, others will need to be processed more deeply over time. It is worth the work! Though your responses will undoubtedly morph as the years go by, the intentional asking, reflecting on, then living of your responses to these questions will lead to a more vital life. The questions can also be fruitful conversation starters for friendships that you hope will deepen.

Finally, you will also notice practices at the end of each chapter. These simple practices may help you more fully integrate God's energy into your life. With all spiritual practices, the goal is not simply to do them. The hope is that they become pathways for you to open yourself up to the creative energy of God's Spirit. So, choose which ones will be important for you and let them, over time, become part of the natural rhythms of your life.

Yes, living a life filled with vitality is possible. But it takes intention. In a world programmed for mind-numbing busyness, quick-fix remedies and soul-shriveling pursuits of more, this book calls you back to the creative and renewable energies of God. The wellspring of these energies is evident in the creation story and accessible for those willing to open themselves to these currents of love and hope. My prayer is that readers of this book will awaken to the power available to them and be surprised by the joy of creative life change.

Practice

Self-awareness is a critical step in any process of change. It helps us establish a baseline of where we are before we move toward where we want to be. Using the themes of this chapter, spend a day or two paying close attention to your life, and then respond to these questions: When did you experience God's energy? What circumstances made you feel most alive? How were the three cultural distortions (pace of life, quick-fix mentality, the seduction of more) evident in your day?

one

The Renewable Energy
of the Holy Spirit

As I sat on my couch staring blankly, seeing nothing but gray, I gathered enough energy to reach out for a lifeline—I called my parents. My father and mother have been deeply immersed in the life of the church, my father as a pastor, my mother a writer and teacher. They must have experienced something like what I was experiencing. They would know what to do. They would say the right thing.

My dad answered the phone. "Kai, good to hear from you. What's going on?" The familiar resonance of his voice ushered me, unwittingly, into the unfamiliar wilderness of my pain. I had hoped to speak rationally and unemotionally about a life, my life, with its emotional and spiritual EKG registering barely a blip. But his voice reminded me of home, a home where I had been loved for who I was, not what I produced. I wanted, on many levels, to be home.

I broke. Tears streamed down my face, careening through newly developed age lines, depositing their salty sadness in the corners of my quivering mouth, as I led my dad into the sanc-

tuary of my discontent: mounting pressure as I assumed the role
of lead pastor; bitter conflict over an unresolved building program
and leadership change; diminished personal energy as I sought
to meet the mounting demands of my working wife, my children
growing into their teens, my expanding and straining congregation, and my leadership in the larger community.

I suspect now what I wanted him to tell me was, *It will be
okay. Go get some rest. Keep moving forward. You can't be everything to everyone. We love you.* Instead, he said, "You may have to
muddle through this for a while."

What? I inwardly cried out. *Put mom on the phone. She'll tell
me I'm awesome and she loves me no matter what!* Outwardly I
stifled a few gasps and breathed a little deeper. I thought about
Dad's words, coming as they did from many years of struggle
through one wilderness after another. I reflected on his present
life and the deep wisdom gained through his experiences, and
I knew, at least for him, there had been life both in and after a
wilderness experience.

The Holy Spirit: God's Creative Energy for Renewal

Dictionary.com defines muddle with these phrases: "to mix-up
in a confused or bungling way," "to make muddy," "to proceed
in an aimless fashion." When I think about muddling, I remember sailing with my friend when I was a kid. One day we
caught a crisp breeze and sailed out into the middle of a large
lake where we lowered the sail and stretched out in the sun's rays.
As the afternoon wore on, the wind died down, and when it
came time to go home, my friend could not remember how to
raise the sail to catch what little breeze there was. So we started
rowing. And rowing. And rowing. Investing all the strength we
had but getting nowhere. That is what muddling feels like to me.

I wonder if, behind his words, my dad was reminding me about a central theme of the faith: it is not all about you, your striving, your efforts. Make some space for God. God might have something to say. God's Spirit might have possibilities for you beyond your narrow imagining. So before we engage the seven renewable energies that add vitality to muddling lives, we need to explore the animating power that pulses through each— God's Spirit.

The power for new or revitalized life comes through the Spirit. The biblical prophet Ezekiel addressed the community exiled in Babylon in a season of desperation. Their temple had been destroyed, leadership dismantled, families divided, land ravaged and people enslaved. Yet he offered hope:

> The hand of the LORD came upon me, and he brought me
> out by the spirit of the LORD and set me down in the middle
> of a valley; it was full of bones. . . . He said to me, "Mortal,
> can these bones live?" I answered, "O Lord GOD, you know."
> . . . "Thus says the Lord GOD to these bones: I will cause
> breath to enter you, and you shall live." (Ezek 37:1-5)

The Spirit of God, God's breath, revives dry bones, reinvigorates dull lives and revitalizes once dead dreams. The apostle Paul refers to this new vitality as strength for the inner being: "I pray that, according to the riches of his glory, he may grant that you may be strengthened in your inner being with power through his Spirit" (Eph 3:16). This new vitality, this strength for our inner being, manifests itself in very ordinary ways, animating our everyday lives and decisions, enabling us to

- get out of bed when we do not know why, brush the stale night film off our teeth and show up for our day

- be surrounded by the inane chatter of our world and resist the impulse to throttle someone
- hear the voice of a friend reminding us that we are not alone
- join in the laughter of a child echoing the delight God takes in creating silly and ordinary wonder
- weather the bleak cycle of winter knowing that it is pregnant with the possibilities of spring
- recall stories of personal courage that inspire a hopeful future

God's Spirit awakens you in the morning, strengthens you for the work of the day and embraces you through the night of restorative sleep.

Though this renewable energy of the Spirit is available to all, it must clearly be stated that there are personal circumstances when we, for any number of reasons, struggle with receiving its life-animating benefits. Clinical depression is real and debilitating. Addictions are pervasive and paralyzing. Grief can deaden the soul and immobilize the body. For those caught in any of these common vice grips of living death, no amount of simple practices or positive platitudes will suffice. In those cases, the encouragement to receive professional help may be the greatest gift of the Spirit that we can offer or receive.

The Holy Spirit in Creation

The Spirit's work has never been and never will be confined to the institution of the church. As we integrate the concept of the Spirit of God as the animating force not only for human creation but also for the entire created order, we are better able to access the energy of the Spirit. By expanding our understanding of the Spirit's presence and work, we also become more intimately connected with the life force of God that energizes the rhythms of our daily lives. Consider the following questions:

- Is it possible for you to imagine God's Spirit infusing you, even in the most ordinary parts of your day?

- Is it possible for you to imagine God's Spirit embracing your family in times of joy or conflict, health or death?

- Is it possible for you to imagine God's Spirit invigorating you in your workplace, whether it is a boardroom or a classroom, whether you work with a laptop or at a cash register?

- Is it possible for you to imagine God's Spirit enveloping and encouraging your neighbor, whether friend or enemy?

- Is it possible for you to imagine God's Spirit enlightening and cherishing peoples of diverse races, creeds, socioeconomic class or other differences?

- Is it possible for you to imagine God's Spirit moving in the mountains and valleys, flowing in the springs and arid deserts?

- Is it possible for you to imagine God's Spirit urging us to care for those mountains and valleys, those springs and deserts?

If the Spirit of God is ever present, then our task is not to bring God's Spirit and power to others but to avail ourselves of its energy, celebrate it and help others to open themselves to its presence in their lives.

The Spirit of Jesus: God's Energy of New Creation

The Spirit of God is the animating force for all of creation. That is good news for us as we consider our inherent connection both to each other and to the whole created order.

The Spirit of God is also embodied uniquely in the person of Jesus Christ. As a follower of Jesus, I trust that the Spirit's power invites us to participate in Jesus' story. "The angel said to [Mary], 'The Holy Spirit will come upon you, and the power of the Most High will overshadow you; therefore the child to be born will be holy; he will be called Son of God'" (Lk 1:35).

When we focus on the narrative of Jesus through the Gospels we see a man free from the oppression of the religious laws and regulations of his day, though he honored them. He interacted openly with all who were willing to share a meal, touch his garments or even climb a tree to see him. None of the trappings of his world—including religious boundaries, socioeconomic class, gender or the expectations of religious people—prevented him from extending a hand of service, offering forgiveness or giving his life. The vitality of the Spirit permeated his being, giving him the right words to say, the power to heal, the strength to care for himself by going away to pray.

Imagine, for a moment, that kind of life—a life of personal freedom and practical hospitality, of reckless generosity and radical compassion, of self-giving service and sacrificial love to all. It is possible. In fact, it has been hard wired into you from the very beginning by your loving Creator. Your responsibility is simply to avail yourself of the Spirit's transforming power.

In the days following my emotional and spiritual crash, I mostly kept to myself. I was not sure what to say or who to trust. I had no idea if anything would change anyway. During a gathering of pastoral colleagues, I was introduced to a simple form of prayer that would become another lifeline for me. The leader called it a breath prayer, and she carefully led the gathering into the process.

"First, find a place without distractions and sit comfortably, your feet on the floor or, better yet, the ground, your hands relaxing on your knees either palms down or facing upward.

"Then, let your eyelids fall and begin breathing more and more deeply, relaxing the body and quieting the mind. As thoughts come, which they will, gently let them pass, refocus on breathing, and relax. If something urgent comes to mind, jot it down and return to this method of prayer.

"After you feel relaxed in body and quiet in mind, think about something in your day that is causing you stress—maybe a meeting with your board or a confrontation with one of your kids—and name the energy you need for that particular situation. Then pray this prayer over and over again saying, 'Spirit of God' as you inhale, and then as you exhale say, 'restore my love,' or 'give me patience' or 'infuse me with energy.' Breathe this prayer over and over again until you feel yourself relaxed in regard to that particular situation."

I wish I could say this one exercise changed my life. It did not. I wish I could say I faithfully practiced this prayer as I had been encouraged to do. This is also untrue. But periodically, I would find myself stopping for small moments of breath prayer when in the past I would have just kept pressing on.

Then, one day, when I was again counseling someone whose life was riddled with problems and I felt my energy flagging and my compassion slipping away, I remembered the prayer. I breathed the words "Spirit of God" on my inhale, and as I exhaled I whispered, "restore my focus." Next breath, "Spirit of God, give me patience." Later in our meeting, "Spirit of God, bless me with compassion." This simple attention to breath, those simple prayer words, allowed me to be present with this man for an hour, honoring him by honoring his pain and giving him the time and space to recharge his life energy.

Over time, this prayer suggestion did become my daily morning practice. Rather than charge through my list of prayer demands for God, demands that depleted my energy by simply reminding me of all my anxieties and worries, I would take a breath, notice it, then take another and let the energy of God enter and encourage me for the day ahead. I was re-learning what I had often taught others. Personal change does not come in dramatic, instantaneous movements forward but small steps taken intentionally and consistently over time.

Practice

Prayer is as simple as taking an intentional breath and claiming that breath as Spirit energy, giving us what we need for the situation or the day. Begin stopping, noticing your breath and making it your prayer.

two

The Energy of Grace

I muddled through the ensuing days and weeks. Passing moments of levity surprised me, allowing me to glimpse the more vital life I had known, though they were few and far between. Mostly I kept pressing into the fog my life had become, a slow-motion journey leading nowhere. The familiar streets of my community narrowed, the familiar rhythms of work put a stranglehold on my soul, the superficial banter of community members sucked the life out of me.

Recalling my dad's words, "You may have to muddle through this for awhile," filled me with disdain for his insensitivity. Why couldn't he have been more helpful, more positive, more forward looking? I had called him to feel better. Why couldn't he fix it, fix me, fix anything? Yet gradually I began to understand. I wasn't alone. He had traversed similar journeys and emerged refreshed and alive. So could I.

In a parallel process to my inner journey, the congregation I served had hired a consultant to help navigate the shifting cultural paradigms both externally and internally. Little did I know, the consultant's best work would be focused on me.

"You look tired," the consultant said after a meeting. "Let's talk." A brief conversation turned to an hour of therapy.

"I am not sure I can do this any more," I confessed. All the external indicators of my work were positive. After twelve years as a staff pastor, I had been asked to assume the role of lead pastor. I was serving a community in the top one percent of worship attendance in the Evangelical Lutheran Church in America and working with a competent long-term staff. I was gaining respect as a community leader and expanding my network of influence both within my tradition and beyond. Yet I was dead inside.

The conversation then wove through a lifetime of strong leaders that I had respected and admired in the church such as my father, my former colleague and other senior leaders who had grown significant ministries. "But I am not like any of them," I said. "The more I try to be, the more conflicted I feel."

Enter the word of grace. "You need to figure out who you are, not who you think you should be."

At first, I did not absorb the transformative implications of his statement. "I need a solution, not guiding wisdom," I muttered to myself and thought, *That's it? That's all you have for me? What are we paying you for?* Yet, upon reflection and over time, the guidance proved priceless. I would never be my father, never have the specific gifts of pastors I admired, but—and this was new—I recognized my own gifts for leading.

It was as if he had given me a new set of glasses to wear. My old ones were, of course, more comfortable, and I caught myself reaching for them from time to time, especially when difficult decisions arose, but the new ones gave me a clarity of vision I had not had before. I saw myself and my life differently—through the lens of love and acceptance, the lens of grace.

As long as I kept them on, I could shed the crushing weight

of what the community expected from me and break free from the strangling grip of my own unrealistic expectations. Infused with this new vision and new energy I began to walk more freely, knowing I was loved and accepted by God no matter what.

Other traditions might describe my experience as being born again. But I say simply I rediscovered the wellspring of the renewable energy of God's grace, a grace that would allow me to accept myself for who I am and empower me to become more authentically who God made me to be.

Grace Is Where It All Begins

"In the beginning . . . God created the heavens and the earth" (Gen 1:1). The cosmos, the natural world and the fullness of our lives come as a gift of God's grace. We have done nothing to deserve or earn it. Our intellect, emotions, the ability to produce and create, the desire for good and the propensity for evil contribute to the mystery of what it means to be part of God's creation, to be in relationship with God, to be human. It is not our right. We are not entitled to life. Life is gift. Life is grace.

Imagine for a moment what it might be like to live without the weight of earning respect, the burden of producing results and the bondage of proving ourselves. That freedom flows from the energy of grace. We can "learn the unforced rhythms of grace" and "learn to live freely and lightly" (Mt 11:28-30 *The Message*). Yet our desire for receiving this energy is strangely limited. Instead of reveling in grace, we choose to live under the weight and burden of someone else's expectations or our own distorted expectations. Thus we constrict the Spirit, binding ourselves to a life of frustration, which often causes us to plummet into destructive life patterns.

At the heart of the struggle for receiving this energy of grace is our image of God. What do we really believe about God and our place in God's universe? Do we believe God is for us or against us? Is God present or distant? Do we matter at all? Our answers to these questions form the architecture upon which the rest of our life is designed.

ESSENTIAL LIFE QUESTION

What is my image of God?

Growing up in a pastor's family as I have, images of God and a father who is a spiritual leader often get intertwined and thus messy. Am I trying to please God or my dad? Is it God who is upset with me, or did I just anger my dad? If I do not feel accepted by my dad, does God lean the same direction?

As a teenager, I would frequent the county fair each year, avoiding all the rides because of my propensity for motion sickness but dominating all the fair games, cashing in on the tacky prizes, from the grossly oversized stuffed gorillas to the pervasive, personalized, plastic trinkets touting the family virtues of the local country fair on one side and a "Made in China" label on the other. One year I was particularly proud of a T-shirt I won that proclaimed, "Jesus is coming . . . and is He pissed!" It was a miracle shirt for me. At one time I could be both religious (it named Jesus, right?) and naughty (we were not supposed to use that language) wearing that shirt.

Beyond the religious shock talk of the words, the shirt made a theological assertion—God, through Jesus, is angry with us! Frankly, at that point in my life I tended to agree. Though my dad had preached about the grace of God since my earliest memory, I wondered whether God was, in reality, just waiting to get me. How could God be pleased with the way I was selling myself short and underachieving in school and in life? How could God accept a messed up party kid nursing a hangover while playing "Jesus Christ Is Risen Today" on his trumpet for Easter sunrise service?

I remember sporting that T-shirt one day as my dad and I were driving to school. I did not mention the shirt, hoping that he would notice it, that he would notice me. With the journey almost complete and no words spoken, I grudgingly broke the silence and asked, "Dad, did you see what my shirt says?" I assumed because it mentioned Jesus that he would be impressed.

He was not.

"Yes, I did." he replied. "But I don't agree. I don't think Jesus is angry with us. I think Jesus loves us, sometimes in spite of ourselves."

His soft-spoken conviction struck like a lightening bolt, piercing my calloused mind and heart. I began to question, what if God could love me, did love me, in spite of myself? At the time, I could not comprehend how life changing that insight would be for me.

Consider another image of God. While conversing with a student in the Renovaré Institute for Spiritual Formation, the topic of our image of God took center stage. Throughout the week we had immersed ourselves in the image of friendship with Jesus. As we talked about how that image resonated with us, the student spoke both of his delight in the image and the struggle of leaving his childhood image of God behind. Throughout his childhood he had pictured God as an enormous being suspending a massive rock over his head. At any moment, any slip-up, the rock would drop and crush him.

I am becoming more and more convinced that our response to the question, What is your image of God? is the essential question for our lives. Whether we actively reflect on it or not, our image of God defines who we are and how we see the world. In fact, we might think about it as the hard drive that runs our lives' operating systems.

- If God is angry, we seek to appease or flee. We live life looking over our shoulder, waiting for the next shoe to drop, or being risk averse, avoiding failure at all costs.

- If God is judgmental, we seek to please God and win a favorable judgment. We live our lives as if we are in an eternal beauty pageant: incessantly proving, promoting and posturing for the prize.

- If God is distant, we can become ambivalent about God and live life on our own even though we are plagued by the nagging question, Is this all there is?

- If God is indifferent, we can be apathetic about a meaningful purpose for our lives and indifferent to the lives of others. We live in constant pursuit of our own pleasure without regard for the rest of the world.

As you can see, the implications of our image of God pervade our lives. Unfortunately, most of the people I encounter inside and outside the faith community have at some point in their lives experienced, been taught, or heard about a God who is angry, judgmental, distant or indifferent. Even when we hope God is gracious and loving, we live as if we have something to prove to God, to others, to the world. Is it any wonder that many have fled their faith communities and, in some cases, abandoned the faith altogether?

For a moment, imagine this:

- What if God is loving?

- What if God is merciful?

- What if God is accessible?
- What if God is compassionate to us and toward the world in times of suffering?

What would your life be like if this was your image of God? I don't know what it would be like for you, but I can confidently say that for me, embracing this image of God as reflected in the person of Jesus revitalized my life. I released the crushing, unrealistic expectations others had placed on me and I had laid on myself. I realized that failure at work or in relationships was not an end but an opportunity to rethink and reimagine. I cut out the fear that I was not enough, inserting in its place the faith that God had, could and would redeem my failures and mistakes.

Having received the energy of grace, I more freely offered it to others. Because I had become more aware of my failings, I was able to release others from my judgment. Because I had a new image of the connective power of grace, I could seek common ground with others, discovering common hopes, striving toward our common dreams for the world.

ESSENTIAL LIFE QUESTION

How does my image of God affect the way I see the world, others, my own life?

Comparison Fatigue

I wish I could say that since that conversation with my dad as a teenager and the conversation years later with our consultant, I have lived my life on this more loving, more grace-filled plane. Some days I just forget and slide into habitual ways. Some days I intentionally toss out those glasses and put on my old ones because I want to feel angry, judgmental or superior. I suspect you know what I am talking about.

Instead of being content with what we have, anxiety over what we do not have makes us fall prey to the seduction of more and drives a sense of discontentment. Instead of recognizing the gift of who we are and being satisfied, we obsess over who we are not, and dissatisfaction corrupts the operating systems of our lives. In the process, our minds and our spirits are distorted by this need to compare, a need none of us can completely avoid.

Comparison fatigue takes hold. The renewable energy of grace is traded in for the destructive energies of relational and material greed, where our misplaced longing for what we do not have or what we are not blinds us. We feel no gratitude for the lives we have been given and the connective love that permeates the created universe.

We might feel fine about ourselves until, mindlessly scrolling through Facebook or Instagram or other social media, we discover that our lives are not nearly as interesting as other people's lives: our vacations pale in comparison, our children are not as cute or successful, our status updates not nearly as funny or interesting. In fact, the growing research on the effects of social media continually points to the paradox that the more connected we are to our devices, constantly scrolling through our social media, the lonelier we are and the less content we are with our own lives.

We might feel okay about the place we live until we watch HGTV and recognize that no one wants to live in a place with popcorn ceilings, devoid of an open-concept living space and featuring bathrooms without a spa tub.

Finally, who can compete with the airbrushed images that adorn billboards, magazine covers, television and the Internet? If our reference point is primarily external, we doom ourselves to lives of anxiety, striving after wind and comparison fatigue.

Unfortunately, the practice of some forms of Christianity can add weight rather than freeing us for our daily living:

- We create morality lists (what is right and what is wrong) to compare ourselves to others.
- We slip into self-righteousness when we have fewer check marks on our list than someone with whom we live or work.
- We let guilt drag us into lives of dutiful obedience rather than letting grace invite us into a life of delight.
- We shackle our souls with fear, trapping ourselves in inactivity, rather than letting the love of God energize our souls, making us eager for the work of our day.

Yet the heart of the Christian witness establishes an alternative to life-constricting, soul-shriveling forms of religion, even those cloaked in Christian language and form. Jesus understood the oppressive weight of religion. In Matthew's Gospel, he confronts the religious leaders with the burden they heap on those who follow their religious structure and rules and invites all to a radically free journey of faith.

> Are you tired? Worn out? Burned out on religion? Come to me. Get away with me and you'll recover your life. I'll show you how to take a real rest. Walk with me and work with me—watch how I do it. Learn the unforced rhythms of grace. I won't lay anything heavy or ill-fitting on you. Keep company with me and you'll learn to live freely and lightly. (Mt 11:28-30 *The Message*)

The renewable energy of grace, our need for it and our resistance to it, is the great equalizer of human experience. Since God knows the core of our being, we cannot hide behind status, accomplishment or lineage. We have only our imperfect, flawed selves to offer to the world. Yet that is the miracle and mystery of grace. Author Anne Lamott writes, "I do not at all under-stand the mystery of grace—only that it meets us where we are but does not leave us where it found us."[1]

When we see ourselves as God sees us, through the lens of grace, we can accept our place in this world, acknowledge our gifts and acquire the capacity to become what we are meant to be. I hope this reality fills you with a sense of identity and be-longing (you are God's) and energizes you with new possibility (your life matters).

And if this is true for you, through the God who created you, then it is also true for all who are created by this gracious God. Jew. Christian. Muslim. Buddhist. Atheist. Black. White. Brown. Male. Female. Young. Old. Gay. Straight. Rich. Poor. Healthy. Sick.

Pause for a moment and let that sink in.

New Eyes to See

Through God's grace we are intimately connected to the web of humanity and all creation. Setting aside the question of eternal salvation, of who is in and who is out, can we imagine what it would be like to see the world as God sees it, through the lens of grace?

One of the great tragedies of the human condition is our pro-pensity to hate others and to use violence against them. Then we rationalize and justify our actions with our image of a vengeful God: the violence inflicted on the Canaanites who inhabited the Promised Land, on Christians by the Romans, on Muslims and Turks during the crusades, on Christians by Christians in the Hundred Years' War following the Reformation, on Native Americans by foreign nations claiming their land, on Jews and others by the Nazis, and up to the present time in our history. Each side claims the primacy of their ideology and image of God.

Each side rationalizes violence in the name of their God.

Is it possible for us to imagine a different kind of world? Is it possible for us to begin to see, through the lens of grace, the beauty of humanity in all its forms? Is it possible to live confidently in our story as followers of Jesus and, at the same time, respect the humanity of those who live another story?

Frank Laubach, in his book *Letters by a Modern Mystic*, helps open our eyes. Laubach was a Christian missionary in the 1930s in the Philippines. His faith in Jesus compelled him to live and serve among the Moros people in an alien land, with a language foreign to his native tongue and a religious system (Islam) that he was yet to appreciate. They did not respect his spiritual journey, and he did not understand theirs.

Over months of growing frustration, Laubach sought sanctuary on Signal Hill through extended periods of solitude and prayer. The journey led him deeper into the heart of God and more intimately connected him with the people he served. He articulated one of his transformative insights in this way: "They must see God in me, and I must see God in them. Not to change the name of their religion, but to take their hand and say, 'Come, let us look for God.'"[2] Consider the implications of Laubach's transformative insight.

First, "they must see God in me." Laubach understands that any witness to God must be an embodied witness. Others need to see God working in him. This insight is particularly prescient in a culture increasingly indifferent to Christianity. Given the number of Christian leaders who have behaved immorally and unethically and the high-profile Christian leaders who spew hate messages toward anyone that does not adhere to their script, and given the emerging generational apathy toward institutions and the growing number of people who claim no religion at all, we are called to respond to Laubach's invitation. He proclaims an embodied witness, which reminds us that the credibility of our words is weighed heavily against the love-ability of our lives. If it does not change anything about me, why would anyone else want to follow? They must see God in me.

Second, "I must see God in them." That might be a stretch for many of us. But consider this: when an artist creates, some part of the artist resides in each of his or her creations. This is true for all of us. Think back to your earliest years when you were asked to write or create something. What was it like for a teacher or another student to critique your work? It was likely painful! Why? They were not just pointing out something that was wrong with your project; instead, it felt as if they were highlighting something that was wrong with you. You poured yourself into that project. The red highlighter pen did not just highlight a mistake. It drew blood! The same is true with a God who creates each of us. Mysteriously, beautifully, some part of God's graciousness is embedded in each person through the very act of creation. Can we see that? If so, how does that affect the way we see others, whether we judge them as like us or different, with us or against us, friend or enemy?

Third, can we meet each other at the intersection of our common humanity and then extend a hand for the common journey? For followers of Jesus, our story has sometimes gotten in the way, but other times it has become the pathway for these connective conversations. Throughout the Scriptures, faithful people struggled with a spiritual arrogance and sense of entitlement that built walls separating who was in and who was out, who was acceptable and who was not, who was clean and who was unclean. Jesus' embrace of tax collectors and sinners, prostitutes and lepers, women and children both threatened the status quo and expanded the vision of the loving reign of the kingdom of God.

In this way, Laubach's witness is laudable for his time and an appropriate model for our time. We can be both firmly identified as followers of Jesus and common pilgrims with all of humanity journeying through life's essential questions. Can we, as Laubach did, extend our hands to one another and say, "Come, let us look for God"?

Practice

The creation story connects us with the source of our life and reconnects us with the web of humanity, restoring vitality to our very being, a vitality that manifests itself in a deep love of life.

The suggested practice has two parts. Using these simple categories for receiving and extending the grace of God, write or reflect on the presence of God's grace in your life:

- *Grace in:* How was God's grace evident in my life today?

- *Grace out:* How did I extend the grace and acceptance of God to others?

These parts can be done together or separately as you discern they are needed in your life. For instance, if you are struggling with ingratitude or a lack of joy in your life, focus on the first question. If you are having difficulty seeing others as God sees them, focus on the second question.

three

The Energy of Possibility

Following our conversation, the consultant suggested I see a spiritual director, someone he knew and trusted. Although I come from a family of trained spiritual directors and honor the profession and the kind of guidance directors can give, I initially balked. *I've been in ministry more than twenty years. What will she know that I don't already know?* Inwardly and more desperately I was asking, *Why can't I figure this out on my own?* Reluctantly, having gained very little traction on my own initiative, I called the spiritual director and made an appointment.

We spent most of the first visit getting to know one another and charting my emotional and spiritual journey. I analyzed everything I said, every gesture she made and every uncomfortable silence, convincing myself that this was a mistake. I did not really need such a person, and there was little more I could gain from these sessions. (Pastors do not always make the best clients.)

If something was going to happen, I wanted it to happen quickly, but the first session ended unremarkably—though I did notice the pace of my heartbeat relaxing. We prayed together and she led me in a brief exercise that she encouraged me to try:

Thank God for each part of the day. In reviewing the events of the day, ask myself when and how I sensed God was present.

Five to ten minutes a day is all she asked of me.

When I returned a few weeks later, we exchanged pleasantries and then entered a time of quiet to calm our minds and spirits. When I was ready, she asked, "Where do you want to start?"

"I'm fine," I lied. "Everything seems better."

"Tell me more," she gently prodded. I focused primarily on work, since it was easier for me to deal with external issues. She then asked me how the prayer exercise had gone. Squirming, I muttered the first thing that came to my mind. "I didn't have time to do the exercise." As I said this, the awareness of my self-deceit delivered a staggering blow. *I did not have time? Five to ten minutes is all she asked! Who doesn't have five to ten minutes a day?* Then a terrifying series of thoughts flashed through my mind. Everything I wanted to do the previous weeks I had done. What if the real issue was that I did not want to pray? Had no interest in praying. No desire to pray.

That thought shocked me, sending my mind spinning out of control. Was my whole professional life a sham? How could I lead a community of faith or call myself a follower of Jesus? Did I even believe what I had been preaching all these years? My lips began to quiver. My self-reliant façade crumbled, and I wept.

The space between the two of us was filled only by my gasps for air and my internal, self-loathing conversation. *Come on, Kai, get it together!*

When the moment seemed right, she spoke without judgment. We talked for a while about what I was experiencing. As the session drew to a close, she said, "You are carrying a lot of heaviness. You don't need me to add any more. Tell me this: What do you do that gives you joy, that brings life?" It seemed a distant memory, but these things came to mind: conversations over a glass of wine with friends; reading good books for pleasure; experiencing music, visual art or dramas that inspire; living-room time with my wife and kids; playing games as a family.

"Could you possibly do one of those in the next few weeks?" she asked.

"That's possible," I haltingly replied. "Yes. I can do that."

When I left her office, I breathed deeply and reentered my world a little more confidently.

God-Created Possibility

Now the earth was formless and empty, darkness was over the surface of the deep, and the Spirit of God was hovering over the waters. (Gen 1:2 NIV)

The creation story had been told for generations, but most scholars believe it was written down and preserved during the Babylonian exile, a wrenching time of self-doubt and probing introspection for the people of Israel. Yet even in the midst of their hopelessness, possibility emerged as they told and retold the creation narrative—the energy of God's grace that birthed the world and the energy of possibility as God's Spirit hovered over the waters of chaos.

According to Walter Brueggemann, "The 'hovering' suggests an ever-changing velocity and direction, and because God is involved this movement is purposeful. This use of the language of movement . . . suggests creative activity in this verse, a bringing of something new out of a chaotic situation."[1] That is the creative and renewable energy of possibility—the hope of something new arising out of a chaotic situation.

Recall the chaotic situation: the Babylonian exile was a desperate period in Israel's history (sixth century B.C.) when their temple was destroyed by the Babylonians, the Promised Land ravaged and families ripped apart and enslaved in a foreign land. Psalm 137 expresses the communal angst of this time:

> By the rivers of Babylon—
>> there we sat down and there we wept
>> when we remembered Zion.
> On the willows there
>> we hung up our harps.
> For there our captors
>> asked us for songs,
> and our tormentors asked for mirth, saying,
>> "Sing us one of the songs of Zion!"
> How could we sing the LORD's song
>> in a foreign land? (Ps 137:1-4)

The gods of Babylon had seemingly won the day—the promise of land a distant memory, the promise of blessing a shattered dream.

Facing these dark times, the Israelites hearkened back to their Creator, their core story and who they were created to be. As they told this story, the energy of possibility seeped into the living memory, embedding hope into their minds and spirits. If God created the heavens and the earth, God could re-create and renew their lives and their community. If God was present in the chaos of creation, God could be present in the chaos of their lives, designing a hoped-for new order.

The prophets of exile carried this uplifting message to the sagging hearts of the people.

> Thus says God, the LORD,
>> who created the heavens and stretched them out,

who spread out the earth and what comes from it,
who gives breath to the people upon it
   and spirit to those who walk in it. (Is 42:5)

I will cause breath to enter you, and you shall live. (Ezek 37:5)

The days are surely coming, says the LORD, when I will make a new covenant with the house of Israel and the house of Judah. . . .

Thus says the LORD,
who gives the sun for light by day
   and the fixed order of the moon and the stars for light
      by night,
who stirs up the sea so that its waves roar—
   the LORD of hosts is his name. (Jer 31:31, 35)

Each prophetic voice connected the new, emerging reality to the God who created all of reality and who would initiate new possibility. Through the despair and hopelessness of exile, memory sustained the Israelites, and the energy of possibility led them forward.

ESSENTIAL LIFE QUESTION
What hopes shape and give meaning to my life?

Mind the Gap

Last year, I journeyed to London, England, for the first time. Because I had never traveled from Heathrow Airport to the center city, the leaders of the group I was meeting wrote out a meticulous description of how to navigate the Tube, London's train system. From the airport, take the Piccadilly line to Hammersmith Station, exit train, find the District line to Victoria Station, exit train, and always "mind the gap" by stepping carefully from the platform onto the train. The route seemed both ominous and endless for this first-time traveler to the UK.

After purchasing my Oyster card, I pushed through the turnstile, my suitcase crashing against the sidewalls, my carry-on bag plunging from my shoulder to my knees each time I adjusted my suitcase, causing me to stumble into the adjacent, somewhat annoyed traveler who obviously knew where he was going. Arriving on the platform, I took out my directions again. Piccadilly to Hammersmith. Piccadilly to Hammersmith. Immediately, anxiety crept in and I began to wonder, *How will I know which one is the Piccadilly train?* As a train entered the station the mass of travelers pressed in around me, constrained by the invisible wall extending up from the painted yellow line on the platform with the words "Mind the Gap." Decision time. The doors opened as the automated voice called out, "Piccadilly line." Phew.

As the arriving passengers scurried off, the awaiting mass seemed to move as one: mothers grabbing the hands of their children and ushering them across the gap, worldly-wise travelers decisively moving to the open seats. But I was momentarily immobilized by the chaos and confusion. *Is there more than one Piccadilly line? What if I end up lost in a strange city? Why couldn't I have someone grab my hand and lead me across the gap? Why didn't I know more about where I was going?* Paralyzed by indecision, I shuddered as the doors began to close.

I wonder how many of us feel like we are stuck on the platforms of our lives—paralyzed by indecision, doors slamming shut all around us. We find ourselves at a place in life where we have become voyeurs to the exciting journeys everyone else seems to be taking or reluctant travelers not knowing which train we should board or unwilling to risk crossing the gap that leads to our next destination. The crowds of people stream past us, each seemingly well-directed and purposeful in action and destination, while we remain paralyzed in our self-doubt, motionless and afraid.

I remember that point in my personal journey when I was so overwhelmed by what I should be doing or what everyone else seemed to be doing that I was afraid to do anything at all. Decisions were unbearable. Relationships were kept at a distance because I did not want anyone to sense my emotional and spiritual inertia. I would not have known the right train to get on even if it stopped in front of me.

Throughout that time, I noticed that the questions asked of me by my spiritual director were far more important than the answers given to me:

- What are you really afraid of?
- What is keeping you from stepping across the gap?
- If you could go somewhere, anywhere, where would it be?
- What decisions would you need to make to hop on that train?
- What implications would those decisions have on your life?

The questions helped me pay attention not only to where I was, my current platform, but also what it would take to cross the gap and step onto the train—any train—that would lead to a new destination.

It seems clear to me that the mindful discernment required for moving from our current platform to our next train has been co-opted for many in our culture by a mindless pursuit of more and different and novel. We have become experience junkies, so disconnected from delight in ourselves and our own lives, on whatever platform we stand, that we leap from train to train, exploring new experience upon new experience because the high of the previous experience wears off more quickly as our dependency on external stimulation deepens.

On the other hand, some of us are so paralyzed by fear of something new, by terror of making the wrong choice, by dread of the unknown journey, that we unquestioningly attach ourselves to the status quo. This is my life. This is all there is. We stand firmly on our platform never allowing ourselves to wonder about the new possibility awaiting us if only we will step across the gap.

As opposed to our addictive tendencies or the inertia of the status quo, the energy of God's possibility calls us to take the time and energy required to claim the platform on which we stand—both the value of being there and the value of moving on—clarify the destination we want to venture toward, and clearly identify both the risks and the rewards of minding the gap and stepping into our future.

Making the Possible, Possible

I have been enlivened and humbled over the years by stories of congregational and community members who have overcome seemingly impossible odds and moved on to create a new life. A father and mother crushed by the untimely death of their infant child find a way to press on. A spouse devastated by the betrayal of her husband and near financial ruin regains her step. A high-level executive released from her job and her place in the community reclaims essential parts of her life. A family torn by loss of income, home and status through a struggle with alcoholism simplifies life and experiences new freedom.

I have also been saddened by stories where the throbbing pain of life became unbearable and a person falls into a vortex of despair and, sadly, life ends—sometimes physically, sometimes emotionally, sometimes spirituality. We cannot understand why this happens, yet my faith tells me that these people are yet loved and embraced by a gracious God.

But it is instructive to look at those who survive and go on to thrive and to note the contributing factors that help them step across the gap to the next train. The contributing factors include a combination of the following: inner strength or resiliency; a community, maybe even just one person, who supported them; some sense of a higher power or purpose for their lives; and courage to step forward. This courage to step forward is a byproduct of immersing oneself in the renewable energy of possibility.

St. Francis captures the movement of the renewable energy of possibility. "Start by doing what's necessary; then do what's possible; and suddenly you are doing the impossible."[2] When faced with daunting life circumstances, a common question is, Where do we start? In these circumstances, we are paralyzed by too many voices, and the voices of our culture can become debilitating. When we give in to the seduction of endless possibility we get sucked into a perpetual cycle of discontent as we wait for that next possible train to catch.

St. Francis suggests an alternate starting point: *start by doing what is necessary.* Given the current platforms of our lives, living with the energy of possibility may mean we start by giving ourselves a break and not feeling the pressure to make every moment beautiful and meaningful and profound. God honors and is present in all parts of life, monumental and muddling moments included.

The prophet Jeremiah's words to those in exile provide a framework for us: "For surely I know the plans I have for you, says the LORD, plans for your welfare and not for harm, to give you a future with hope" (Jer 29:11). The people of Israel have a future with God, a hope. What inspiring words. Yet those words were spoken while they were still in exile, still captive, with no apparent timeline for release.

So what should they do while they wait? "Build houses and live in them; plant gardens and eat what they produce. . . . But seek the welfare of the city where I have sent you into exile, and pray to the LORD on its behalf, for in its welfare you will find your welfare" (Jer 29:5-7). Do what you can now to build your own strength, build family and relationships, and build the community. In other words, before you can know what your future will look like, take care of the present. In fact, what you do in the present, and how you do it, will open up your future. Start with what is necessary.

Following our meeting, I took my spiritual director's advice and identified one life-giving experience that I would find time to do. I decided to allocate two hours of uninterrupted time to walk up and down the sidewalks of the Short North, an artsy district on High Street in Columbus, Ohio, phone turned off, and simply gaze into the art shops, noticing the beauty and reflecting on the creativity. Or thinking about nothing at all.

What an amazing time. It was so simple, yet it shifted my thinking in two key ways.

First, I had gotten myself to the point where I could not imagine living differently. I was bound by a schedule, by the demands of work and relationships, and that was just how it was going to be. Suck it up. Gut it out. But, in fact, I discovered I had more power of choice than I imagined.

Second, I had too narrowly defined what was spiritual. In my mind, spiritual activities were activities like prayer and Bible study, worship and service—activities during which you purposefully think, reflect and respond to God. I had not conceptualized such an ordinary activity as window gazing in the Short North as spiritual. Yet our spiritual life is our life. All of our lives are lived as an active response to God's grace. By reframing the question, my spiritual director helped me reimagine what was possible and reminded me, "Kai, you have the courage to do it."

Contemporary studies confirm the power of this focused imagining or reimagining for our lives. Creativity researcher Ruth Richards notes, "It is significant that when we imagine something, our brains can react just as if we were encountering the situation itself. This potential provides us with real power."[3]

Visualization, however, is only one step. Pianists visualize their performance, but then they must play. Runners visualize their race, but then they must tie up their laces and run. Swimmers imagine each stroke, each turn, but then they must get in the pool and swim.

The people of God imagined something new in their lives, even when their present reality dictated otherwise, and then they stepped off their platform, crossing the gap toward their unknown destination. A critical step in opening up new possibility for our lives is finding the courage to act. Then we can allow this focused, intentional acting to change perceptions about ourselves and open up new possibilities for creative life change.

ESSENTIAL LIFE QUESTION

What life resources give me the strength and the courage to act?

Integrity and Intention

A few years ago I received the following email from a young physician who is a member of the congregation I serve: "I was working in a laboratory full time, doing a clinical research project, seeing patients, moonlighting (usually between 11:00 p.m. and 5:00 a.m.), then going right back to work. . . . As I let the pressures of life mount, I realized that my previous coping skills . . . were not working." He wrote about a recurring and debilitating thought that he was failing at his job and his relationship with his wife and child, and that his compassion for his patients was minimal. After consultation with another physician he decided that he would put two specific actions into place.

First, he would meditate every day, quiet his mind and spirit, and renew his focus and energy for all his relationships.

Second, as he approached his daily interactions he would consciously ask himself, *Am I encountering this relationship with integrity and intention?* He later wrote that living this way has been "extremely powerful for my life," and that these two specific actions have been "wonderful spiritual tools."

Integrity and intentionality are key components to the renewing energy of possibility. Integrity ensures that our chosen platform and hoped-for destination are consistent with who we are. Intentionality moves us to purposeful reflection and action. We step across the gap.

One of the stumbling blocks we trip over in deciding how to cross the gap is the well-intentioned but self-referential advice of those around us. It sounds like this: "When I was in a similar situation, I did this . . . I think you need to try it." "This always works for me. I'm sure it will work for you." Or, "It has been a few weeks now; shouldn't you be getting better?" Well-meaning, yes. Helpful, not necessarily. What is helpful to some may or may not be equally helpful to you. Know that. Do not berate yourself for boarding a different train than others have taken.

I was often envious of the contemplatives I knew who loved

solitude and could seamlessly move from the chaos and clutter of this world to a rich, renewing period of quieting their mind. So, I decided, since it worked for them, it should work for me. I would go and find a place to be alone, sit quietly and drive myself crazy. My fingers would be drumming after five minutes. Instead of quieting my mind, the quiet time opened up the floodgates of critical self-talk: *First I could not figure out how to get my life together, and now I cannot even sit still with myself for five minutes.* Though I have subsequently discovered the value of quiet and solitude, a subject to which I will return in the chapter on rest, this false start for renewal forced me to ask the questions, How am I uniquely wired? and, What exercises are integral and life giving to me?

I am an extrovert. I gain energy from people, especially when engaged in purposeful conversation. Even when I write, I write in coffee shops, surrounded by people and commotion, alone with my Pandora music plugged into my ears but never alone. I also need to have my body engaged in the spiritual formation process. Physical exercise and movement are critical for my well-being. That is why, instead of retreating to my spiritual cave to be alone with God, walking up and down streets, engaging others through their cre-

ESSENTIAL LIFE QUESTION

Am I an extrovert or an introvert? What life-giving practices might work for me?

ative work, is life giving. I have found this to be true for others who, like me, are extroverts trying to grow spiritually. Books published about spiritual practices are often written by introverts and focus on spirituality for introverts. Extroverts need a different way of expressing their spirituality.

Though I now know there is value in introspective times of withdrawal and quiet prayer, I often felt like I had jumped on the wrong train. What made me most alive was engagement, not disengagement. When I reframed the purpose of these practices to include not only the question, How do I experience the presence of God? but also, What are the activities that God's Spirit can use to make me most alive? then I began to experience the breadth of God's love infusing all parts of my life.

For instance, I used to see my physical workouts as separate from my life with God, something I did because I liked to do it. Now I envision them as strengthening my body for the work I have been given. Weight lifting is a spiritual exercise for me. Sitting on the sidelines of my kids' athletic events was an exercise in patience. Now I envision it as an opportunity to be with others in ordinary time and build community. Nights out with friends, filled with good food and conversation, were just that: nights out. Now they are times to appreciate those who share the platform we are sharing and be sensitive to those, including myself, who might need to cross the gap and head out in a new direction.

When we identify practices that uniquely connect us with the wellspring of God's energy, we tap into the renewable energy of possibility. Putting one foot in front of the other, we step off our current platforms, cross the gap, and confidently entrust our new journey to the hands of our God, living as if all God promised was true. Rabbi Brad Hirschfield writes,

> That as-if-ness is an amazing thing. We love our children and our parents as if they haven't disappointed us. We love our spouses as if they haven't hurt or betrayed us. We negotiate treaties as if prior treaties haven't been broken. That's what it means to be idealistic, to be hopeful, to be faithful, to be filled with faith that more is always possible than we first imagined.[4]

Practices

From the beginning, as the Spirit hovered over the waters of chaos, as the fresh wind of Pentecost swept over the disciples, the renewable energy of possibility has sustained, ennobled and mobilized God's people to not only think different but be different. These practices will help awaken you to the possibility already embedded in your day as well as encourage you to move toward the possibility awaiting you in the future.

Daily examen. At the end of the day, take a few minutes and ask these questions: (1) What did I do today that was life giving? Can I find ways to repeat that kind of activity? (2) What did I do that drained life out of me? Can I release that activity? If not, can I find ways to reframe it?

Mind the gap. On a piece of paper, create two columns. The first column reflects your current platform, where you are now. Ask, How will I attend to the reality of my present platform? What is good about this place? What causes anxiety? What needs to be done here before stepping too quickly into another possibility?

The second column represents the new destination, where you would like to be. For this column, ask, What is it about this place that makes me think it will provide better opportunities for me to live fully? What preparation will I need to set out on this new journey? How can I consciously invite God into this new journey? Is there someone to grab my hand and help me cross the gap?

four

The Energy of Paradox

As I wallowed through this time of emotional and spiritual confusion, I often pondered what it would be like to resign my call and change my vocation. Anything seemed better than the painful thought of failing my family, myself and God. In the past, those thoughts led to self-doubt, confusion and anxiety, but this time was different. A new path emerged in which I drew power and direction from a different source. God's grace shielded me from critics and lessened my defeating self-talk. God's voice seeped into my being, reminding me of who I am, what my gifts are, and my unique call to lead. Eugene Peterson's interpretation of Mark 1:11 in *The Message* provided daily respite and encouragement: "You are my [s]on, chosen and marked by my love, pride of my life." More days than not, I actually believed it.

Still, despite my belief that God could and would drag me forward through uncertain, new territory, old questions and doubts remained: What if the community wanted or needed a different kind of leader? What if my staff needed something I could not give? What if public ministry ultimately was not my call? What would I do? How would I support my growing family and put my kids through college? What would others think?

Months into this journey, I took what felt like a big risk and preached a sermon series using my own story of self-doubt and despair followed by creative life change as a parallel storyline to God's desire and capacity to release us from our barren, wilderness lives (Is 40:3). Not everyone understood and was willing to receive it. I overheard one person say, "He just needs to buy a red Corvette and get over his mid-life crisis." I bristled at the comment. On a superficial level, I would have chosen a black Harley Davidson over a red Corvette any day. But the comment reminded me how hard it is to be honest, even in Christian community, and especially as a leader.

Fortunately that dismissive sentiment was not widely held. Most of the cards and emails I received, the quick conversations in the hallway and extended conversations at coffee shops, expressed overwhelming gratitude. A few desired answers to their life questions, but most understood there were few, if any, sufficient pat answers. Some discovered an internal wisdom guiding their decision making. Others found that even though answers were insufficient for all that was happening in their life, they longed for greater connection. New energy flowed into the community as we struggled together with the great paradoxes of life.

Paradox Is Embedded in God's Creation

"Then God said, 'Let there be light'; and there was light. And God saw that the light was good; and God separated the light from the darkness" (Gen 1:3-4). In the first act of creation, God separated light from darkness, but each remained in relationship to the other. Light and darkness both have their place in the order of creation and in the rhythm of life. Claus Westermann writes, "God created the world in such a way that light has a priority. God created the world in such a way that darkness, which is described neither as created by God nor as good, is a necessary part of the created order."[1]

In the story of creation, darkness and light coexist. In the world, darkness and light coexist. In my life and yours, darkness and light coexist. Even if we struggle against that paradox, we know its truth. The experience of joy is more profound having known sorrow. The power of friendship enlivens us more following an experience of loneliness. The freedom of forgiveness releases us after having been gripped by guilt. The promise of new life energizes even when faced with the peril of death.

Parker Palmer, in *The Promise of Paradox*, asserts that paradox constitutes the core teaching of most wisdom traditions:

> The promise of paradox is the promise that apparent opposites—like order and disorder—can cohere in our lives, the promise that if we replace either-or with both-and, our lives will become larger and more filled with light. It is a promise at the heart of every wisdom tradition I know, not least the Christian faith. How else can I make sense of the statement, "If you seek your life, you will lose it, but if you lose your life, you will find it"?[2]

The energy of paradox is released and the bandwidth of our soul expanded when we are forced to face our limitations, immerse ourselves in those tensions and learn, over and over again, that the ultimate power for life comes from God.

The reality of these great paradoxes gives rise to perplexing questions: Does God give us times

ESSENTIAL LIFE QUESTION

What life circumstances have forced me to wrestle with the paradox of light and darkness?

of darkness so that we can experience the light? Where is God in those times of darkness? Are there times when we are outside the realm of God's love and grace? What does this mean for us when we are deep into a dark night or fearing the darkness that is descending?

Philosophers and theologians throughout the centuries have written volumes addressing these haunting paradoxes of life: the reality of suffering and joy, bondage and freedom, death and life. On a more personal level, various forms of these questions have echoed in the lives of people I know and in my own life: Why did I get cancer? Why did this tragic accident happen to me, in my family? If God is a God of joy and life, why am I so joyless and lifeless? How can I believe God is good with all the evil that is happening in the world? Can I believe in God at all given the evil that is happening in the world?

Too often the Christian community, in striving to be relevant and popular, has filed these questions away, choosing to focus on the positive, the uplifting, the pathways to our best life each day, every day, all the time. Barbara Brown Taylor, in her book *Learning to Walk in the Dark,* calls these the "sunny spiritualities,"[3] spiritualities of light and love and laughter that are not designed or equipped to address the realities of many lives.

The unfortunate consequence is that those who are languishing in a loveless, humorless darkness find no comfort or hope for their lives, so they reject that representation of the faith as frivolous and non-connective, or they abandon the faith altogether. Without a rugged faith that embraces both light and darkness, health and pain, death and life, we can easily walk away, because that representation of the faith does not deal with the reality of the world we live in.

The Unwanted Gift

One of the helpful images I was given during my wilderness period came from my mother. She had worked with her sister on a collaborative art show that fused poetry from Denise Levertov, the visual artistry of my aunt and the prose of my mother to co-create a poetic/visual/prose journey from life to death and back to life again—the movement through the dark night of the soul.

One of my mom's musings caught my attention: "Not what we wanted. Not the goal we sought while suffering through dark times. Must we say 'yes' to light and storm, growth and pain? Will we?"

Not what we wanted. Unwanted. An unwanted gift.

Can embracing and living into the paradox of light and storm, growth and pain, be an unwanted gift? Gifts are meant to surprise us, connect us more deeply with the giver and enhance life. Is that also true of unwanted gifts of struggle and pain? Will they surprise us with their redemptive potential? Will they connect us more deeply with one another, with ourselves, with God? Will they enlarge our lives, expand our souls and extend the boundaries of our newly discovered compassion for others, having walked through a common journey of light and storm? Must we say yes?

I now know that is what my dad was alluding to when he said, "You may have to muddle through this for awhile." I hated it when he said those words, but in retrospect, I understand their truth. I discovered something more about my ability to adapt, the limits of my reach, my propensity for self-defeating talk and the expansive capacity of God's grace. I began to learn what I needed and what I should avoid. This time, the painful life experience became a gift, one I had not asked for, one I did not want, but in the end, a gift.

When we receive a gift, our automatic response is to wonder who the giver is. Did God give me this? Did I give it to myself as the result of my own decisions and personality? Did someone else purposefully or randomly give it to me? Perhaps the first truth we need to accept is that often, whether the gift is wanted or unwanted, these questions are unanswerable. We may never know. What has happened is a part of the past that we can neither change nor do over. Our only choice is how we use the gift. Where we go from here. What we do next. The question, Why? becomes, What now? Barbara Brown Taylor captures the paradox well: "I have learned things in the dark that I could never have learned in the light, things that have saved my life over and over again, so that there is really only one logical conclusion. I need darkness as much as I need light."[4]

The story of Jacob in Genesis 32 is one of my favorite stories of a struggle with light and darkness, both internally and externally, that becomes an unwanted gift. Leading up to this story, Jacob's relationship with his brother Esau was severed when he conned Esau out of his birthright and connived with his mother to steal his father's blessing. Esau's rage was white hot and justified. He threatened to kill Jacob for his duplicity, for dishonoring the family tradition of blessing and for heisting his greater portion of the inheritance. Sensing Esau's rage, Jacob fled to a distant land where he lived in exile for two decades.

In verses 22-32, Jacob prepares to meet Esau for the first time since the family fractured. The night before their meeting, Jacob wrestles with and is ultimately blessed by a strange night visitor. Is it God? Is he wrestling with his guilty conscience? Is he wrestling with God and his guilty conscience? My guess is some of both. The upshot of this biblical precursor to the World Wrestling Federation is threefold: (1) Jacob is blessed; (2) his name, Jacob, which in Hebrew means heel, trickster, over-reacher, supplanter,[5] is changed to "Israel," meaning one who wrestles with God and prevails; (3) he bears a limp from that struggle that will mark him forever. The wrestling, though painful, transformed him.

I bet you have been there—wrestling through the night with pressing anxieties, unresolved or unresolvable problems, penetrating questions of who you are and why your life matters or does not. What you probably know from your own experience is that no one can talk you out of that space with positive platitudes. If someone tries, they come off as dismissive of the issue or the person. But having lived within the tensions of life's paradoxes, we can be people who offer ways for others to reframe their circumstances and re-envision their lives.

While no one longs to receive these unwanted gifts of growth and learning, they are integral to life. We do not automatically grow through this kind of suffering. Discerning how life can be different as a result of this unwanted gift requires intentionality of thought, introspection and prayer. These questions might help the discernment: Where is God's presence in this circumstance? What can I learn about myself and my relationships to others? Having had this experience, what can be done differently? How can my experience help others?

ESSENTIAL LIFE QUESTION

In what ways have I been blessed by an unwanted gift?

Must There Be a Reason?

The renewable energy of paradox can be released through your struggle with these unwanted gifts. Though we may, in retrospect, discern a movement of growth through some of life's unwanted gifts, we are also presented daily with suffering that we need to say, very clearly, is not part of God's will or design. The creation story reminds us that "God saw everything that he had made, and indeed, it was very good" (Gen 1:31). While we can never fully know the way darkness and light interweave for good, it is certainly true that some events are not part of that good. In spite of that, as those who follow a crucified and risen God, we cling to the hope that God can somehow redeem and restore all things.

When we attempt to answer the questions of the paradox of good and evil, too often we default to unhelpful religious platitudes that distort God's nature and character. A child dies and someone says, "God must have wanted another flower in the garden or angel in the choir"; a young mother dies of cancer and someone says, "It must be part of God's plan"; a drunken teenager is paralyzed in an accident and we hear, "Maybe this will be a lesson to others."

Though I understand these sentiments are offered largely out of our discomfort—we simply do not know what to say—the underlying assumptions are troubling. Can you imagine a God who designed this world in love, for love, deliberately causing pain and harm to children or families just so that God might have more company in the heavenly realm or so that someone else might learn a lesson? Think for a moment about the implications of that line of thought. Think about the anxiety that would cause in our lives. What prevents us from being next on God's hit list? Are some people's lives expendable so that others can finally learn their lesson?

Many of the *why* questions will forever go unanswered. Let me repeat that: Many of the *why* questions will forever go unanswered. It does not mean we lack faith or knowledge. With all our human capacity to know and explore and discover, we still live under the condition of a limited capacity to plumb the depths of the human heart, the depths of the universe, the depths of God. In those cases, the best response we may have is, *I don't know why.*

If we release the *why* question, our energy is freed to ask other questions: Will we accept an unwanted gift? Will we say yes to light and storm? Can we be people who are willing to embrace the unanswerable questions and stand together with God? Can we be people who are willing to take this mysterious journey with one another?

Taking the Journey . . . Together

The apostle Paul reminds us that when community is functioning as God desires, we "rejoice with those who rejoice, weep with those who weep" (Rom 12:15). We are not alone. We are not alone in our suffering. We are not alone in our hope.

As we struggle together with life's paradoxes—things we do know, things we do not know, things we will never know—I would like to suggest three responses: (1) acceptance—suffering is real and unavoidable, for us and the world; (2) resistance—we are called to stand against suffering that is destructive to ourselves, others and the created world; (3) presence—we do have something to offer even when answers are few. We offer ourselves.

Acceptance. Life is hard. There, I said it. Life is hard. Unfortunately, an exorbitant amount of time, energy and money is spent resisting that reality. Instead of accepting its truth, we avoid it. From parents sheltering their kids from any pain and discomfort, to adults distracting themselves with external pleasures to avoid internal strife, to those anesthetizing themselves with a myriad of addictions to money or alcohol or pornography or affirmation or achievement, many in our culture have become pain avoidant.

Accepting that darkness and light coexist can give us a more realistic perspective. The opening of John's Gospel embraces both that reality and our hope: "The light shines in the darkness, and the darkness did not overcome it" (Jn 1:5). Darkness exists, but it is not the only reality. Those who follow Jesus understand that we live at the intersection of the world that is and the world that can be. God's unconditional love and presence allow us to accept the world that is—the trial and tribulation of it—because we have seen a vision of what the world can be. In this case, acceptance is not denial or an expression of passivity. Acceptance is a way to release our personal control of the outcomes and place ourselves in the hand of the one who, in love and sacrifice, overcame the world.

Acceptance allows us to echo the words of the psalmist, "Weeping may linger for the night, but joy comes with the morning" (Ps 30:5). Though we experience periods of suffering in our lives, we trust that suffering can produce endurance, and endurance can produce character, and character can produce hope, a hope that will not disappoint (Rom 5:3-5).

For followers of Jesus, the cross embraces those paradoxes of life. Parker Palmer writes,

> The way of the cross is a way of absorbing pain, not passing it on, a way that transforms pain from destructive impulse into creative power. When Jesus accepted the cross, his death opened up a channel for the redeeming power of love. When we accept the crosses and contradictions in our lives, we allow that same power to flow.[6]

In accepting the reality of our own crosses, we walk in solidarity with a God who experienced the depths of human suffering and loss through Jesus' death. In accepting our own crosses, we become channels of love to those who desperately need to know they are not alone.

Resistance. One of the valid critiques of followers of Jesus in our contemporary culture is that we have become so intently focused on our personal relationship with Jesus that we can convince ourselves we are being faithful even as we ignore a world desperately in need. Followers of Jesus cannot allow indifference and apathy to overtake them. From the beginning, the ears of God heard the cry of the people when they were enslaved (Ex 2:24), the voice of God railed against the faith community when it became too insular, calling them to greater acts of justice and mercy (Amos 5:24), and the heart of God, revealed in the life of Jesus, expanded the boundaries of God's kingdom of love—dining with tax collectors and sinners, siding with prostitutes, healing the cast-off lepers, and blessing the poor, the imprisoned and all who hunger and thirst.

Faith communities, formed by God's radical kingdom of love, are invited to participate in the restoration of this world, resisting both our hesitancy to get involved and the greater movements of evil that diminish human life, destroy community and devalue the created world. In the well-known words of the Serenity Prayer, we accept the things we cannot change, but we also pray for courage to change the things we can.

Presence. In times of grief and loss, people might remember what you say, but they will always remember your loving presence. I have learned this the hard way. I remember attending a funeral luncheon for a family friend. Their son and daughter-in-law had lost a child in childbirth and were, as you can imagine, beside themselves with grief. I was a college student, unfamiliar with the deep cycles of grief and uncomfortable with the situation itself and my presence in the situation. There came a point during the luncheon when I was standing alone at the buffet table with the bereft father. Every part of me wanted to say the right thing to comfort his aching heart. I searched and searched and searched for the right words, and all that came out was, "This is really a good lunch." He nodded and walked away into his silent sadness.

I kicked myself for weeks, maybe months. Even now, when I think of that moment I cringe. From the accumulated wisdom of years, I now understand that what I thought he needed was probably not what he needed at all. I thought he needed me to be wise and insightful and to say the right thing to help alleviate his pain. I suspect he simply needed to know he was not alone. Would someone, anyone, be willing to show up and be present in his wordless grief? Would someone, anyone, be willing to carry, in whatever way he or she could, some of the unbearable weight of sadness and loss until he had the strength to carry more of it himself? People might remember what you say, but they will always remember your loving presence.

Practices

Rather than bifurcating the world into good and bad, light and dark, can we expand the horizons of our souls by accepting the great paradoxes in life and not so quickly dismissing or avoiding them? When we say yes to both light and storm and embrace the unwanted gift we access the power and renewing energy of paradox.

Memorization. Memorization is an important practice. When we memorize words of the Bible or words of a song or a prayer we allow them to move from our heads to our hearts, eventually becoming part of who we are and how we imagine the world. Subsequently, what we memorize matters.

To immerse yourself in the renewable energy of paradox, consider memorizing one or both of the following. Let them form your mental response to life's great paradoxes.

- The Serenity Prayer: "God, grant me the serenity to accept the things I cannot change, the courage to change the things I can, and the wisdom to know the difference. Amen."

- Romans 5:3-5: "Suffering produces endurance, and endurance produces character, and character produces hope, and hope does not disappoint us, because God's love has been poured into our hearts through the Holy Spirit that has been given to us."

Practice compassion. Identify someone you know who is struggling. Find a way to be present with them. Share a meal. Invite them out for coffee or a drink. Send them a brief note telling them they are in your prayers. Do not worry what to say. Just be present with them in small, consistent ways.

The Energy of
the Natural World

A few years before my emotional and spiritual crash I started pursuing another degree from Fuller Seminary in Pasadena, California. The program required time on campus twice a year for a week or two. Living in Columbus, Ohio, I chose to travel to Pasadena for classes either in late fall or winter. I am no dummy.

As I was slowly emerging from that spiritual wilderness, and in the midst of a particularly grueling Ohio winter, I flew to California for one of my classes. One day, I discovered a small rose garden on campus, surrounded by a grassy knoll. I sat on the grass, stretched out and settled in for a late afternoon study session. Seventy degrees. Ocean-blue skies. Not a cloud in sight. The kind of day in which, when my wife would call from dreary Ohio, straddling a sick kid on her hip while making dinner for the others and would ask, "How's the weather?" I would say, "Oh, it's not too bad."

It was glorious!

As I put my book down for a break, I happened to gaze over at the rose bushes and noticed a single ant traversing the long stem of a rose. Looking closer, I saw the ant was joined by another and another and another. Hundreds of ants swarming around the base of the roses, some burrowing into the soil, others setting off on the harrowing climb up the stem, still others lugging crumbs of food twice their size back to the hill for dispersion in the community.

I was transfixed.

I asked myself, *How have I never noticed this whole world happening in front of me?* The ants burrowing into the ground, aerating the soil so that plants can better take root and grow. The plants converting light energy from the sun into the chemical energy needed to survive and thrive. The whole process of photosynthesis maintaining and supplying oxygen levels that I need to live. My life and the ants' lives intimately connected in the web of creation.

Our Connection with the Natural World

"And God said, 'Let the waters under the sky be gathered together into one place, and let the dry land appear. . . . Let the waters bring forth swarms of living creatures. . . . Let the earth bring forth living creatures.' . . . And God saw that it was good" (Gen 1:9, 20, 24-25). In the biblical tradition, most of the creation story describes the emergence of the natural world, yet most of our thinking, introspection and theologizing is preoccupied solely with humanity.

In the last few centuries during the post-industrial revolution, humans have plundered and ravaged the natural world for the purposes of economic and industrial progress. Today, a growing number of scientists, philosophers, theologians and artists are proclaiming the inevitable peril created by humankind's unquenchable thirst for progress at the expense of the natural world.

This chapter is not intended to be a definitive Christian response to this problem. As I came to understand myself and those around me, I realized that our attitude toward, respect for and love of God's creation affects the state of our minds and souls. When we disregard or even neglect or abuse the created order, we are hurting ourselves and disrespecting the God who cherishes the whole creation. The biblical witness expresses that human life issued forth from the same raw materials as all of creation. The Hebrew people even drew an etymological connection, the first person (*adam*) being formed from the earth (*adamah*) (Gen 2:7).

The intimate connection humankind has with creation is inherent in the creation story. And our responsibility for caring for the creation is a biblical stance, not a political stance (Gen 2:15). When we dishonor and abuse God's creation, we dishonor our relationship with God. Brian McLaren reframes the conversation in light of the biblical command to love our neighbors:

> What kind of world do we want to bequeath to those downstream from us in time? Do we want to deprive our grandchildren from seeing elephants and tigers and hummingbirds in the wild. . . . Do we want to leave them a world even less in balance than our world today? Is that neighborly? The more we as Christians follow Jesus by thinking in terms of our duty to our neighbors "downstream" in space and time, the more we will take our stewardship of creation seriously.[1]

This chapter examines the life lessons provided by the natural world, including beauty (a lesson on how God inspires), dormancy (a lesson on how embracing the natural life cycles of the created world expands our souls) and coexistence (a lesson on the need for interdependence).

Beauty Inspires

Joseph Campbell recounts the following story: "Once a Zen master stood up before his students and was about to deliver a sermon. And just as he was about to open his mouth, a bird sang. And he said, 'The sermon has been delivered.'"[2] Beauty awakens wonder within us, which the Spirit uses to lift our eyes to gaze on the mystery and vastness of God.

Throughout the biblical narrative, the writers point to the natural world as a living classroom where we are educated about the nature of God. The psalmist proclaims, "The heavens are telling the glory of God; and the firmament proclaims his handiwork" (Ps 19:1) and expresses the resonating power of God that infuses all creation. When Jesus teaches about the providential care of God for our lives, inviting us to trust and not be afraid, he uses the natural world as the teacher: "Look at the birds of the air. . . . Consider the lilies of the field" (Mt 6:26, 28). As God cares for and adorns God's creation with splendor, God will also care for you. The natural world is a virtual classroom with the creator God as its primary teacher.

The beauty in the natural world comes in many forms. Each time we open our eyes to see this beauty, we are ushered into an ever-deepening sense of awe over the wonder of creation. In the past, I have been invited to be guest pastor for the weekend on Bald Head Island, North Carolina. The permanent residents of Bald Head Island pride themselves on their connection with nature, the preservation of the natural habitats on the island and the loggerhead sea turtles.

A few years ago, hundreds of people gathered on the beach to watch one of the loggerhead turtle nests being cleaned up after the eggs had hatched. Then, suddenly, a solitary baby turtle emerged, still alive, from the nest. As if by instinct, the people parted and formed an aisle for the baby turtle to paddle its way down the sand, eventually being swept away by an incoming wave.

Later, the island conservationists told the group that it is essential for the baby turtle to feel its way to the ocean and not be picked up by human hands. The process will imprint this exact location into the turtle's memory so that years later, after traveling hundreds of miles up and down the eastern seaboard, the turtle will return to this very spot to lay her eggs. When I heard this my mouth dropped open in disbelief as I considered the Creator's design in the loggerhead turtles and the intricacies, mysteries and simple beauty of nature.

Now it is time for confession. Though the natural world can school me on a beauty that inspires and connects me with the mystery and wonder of God, I often skip class. I mindlessly step on the ants that cross my path, curse the birds of the air as they poop on my car, and drive past the lilies of the field as I speed down my asphalt track to and from my carefully controlled indoor climate at work and at home. One of the curses of the suburban world I inhabit and the fast-paced life I often pursue is that I do not stop long enough to notice, to wonder, to be inspired. Consequently, I cut myself off from the energy of the natural world and the natural beauty that inspires. My loss. What about you?

ESSENTIAL LIFE QUESTION

How can I allow the beauty of creation to inspire me?

Dormancy

While sitting and basking in the beauty of the roses, a gardener walked up. "Do they bloom like this all winter?" I asked. "I've watched the Rose Bowl parade my whole life and have always been astounded by the number and the beauty of the roses, especially while suffering through the winters of the upper Midwest." The man looked at me, surprised at the question, but then explained, "All these living things have seasons of growth and dormancy, so we prune them back in early January. That allows them time to strengthen their root systems before putting all their energy back into blooming."

A former colleague often repeated the common phrase, "Grace grows best in the winter." Intellectually, I understood that winter was a metaphor for those times in life when hope and energy lie dormant, but deep under the surface of life something is happening, something that will begin to grow later. Experientially, however, this saying seemed like a mere platitude when my winter came and my spirit deadened, the days turned bleak and lifeless, and my future appeared as dismal as a cold winter day.

The thing about dormancy in humans is that we doubt it will ever end; we fear we will never bloom again. But when I thought I could endure no more, spring aroused from its slumber and provided the nourishment for new growth. In retrospect, I discovered the wisdom of the phrase, "Grace grows best in the winter."

The changing seasons teach vital life lessons, not just for the long seasons of our lives, but also for each day. Daily dying to bad habits, destructive thoughts and misguided judgments is not just good advice, but an essential time for pruning off counterproductive behaviors and deepening our desire to rediscover the wellspring of God's energy for life. Unfortunately, when we become disconnected from the natural world our capacity to embrace the natural rhythm of growth and dormancy is diminished.

Growing up in a rural community in Minnesota I was far more in tune with the rhythms of the natural world than I am now. My friends would often invite me to work with them on their farms—baling hay at the end of the season, milking the cows in the morning, slopping the pigs during the day. Working alongside my friends, I tapped into the rhythms of their lives through their conversation with one another and their daily experiences. Seasons of abundance were sources of gratitude; seasons of drought threatened their livelihood.

Every year I would be invited to pick rocks in the fields before the cycle of planting and harvesting could begin. Every year I would wonder where those massive boulders came from. Every year my friends would remind me that the natural shifting of the earth pushes up rocks into the field and those rocks need to be found and removed before the plows can go through, the seeds planted and the crop harvested.

In that way, our lives mirror the rhythms of the natural world. A season of necessary dormancy provides the opportunity for our conscious or subconscious boulders to emerge, be identified and removed, which, in turn, opens the way for seeds to be planted and nurtured and the possibilities of new growth to emerge. Grace grows best in the winter.

Coexistence

Daniel Goleman tells a remarkable story about the intimate but largely untapped connection we have with the natural world. In an interview with a researcher studying the Moken tribe, a tribe of sea nomads in Southeast Asia, he discovered this: "Just before the 2004 tsunami swept through the islands they inhabited in the Indian Ocean, the Moken 'realized the birds had stopped singing and the dolphins were swimming farther out to sea. . . . So they all climbed in their boats and traveled to deep ocean, where the tsunami crest was minimal as it passed them. Not one Moken was hurt.'"[3] Stunning. I barely know when a thunderstorm is coming until I am drenched with rain, and they sensed, through their intimate connection with the patterns of the birds and dolphins, a tsunami was imminent. They took action, and it saved their lives and their culture.

If we pay attention, we must humbly acknowledge our utter dependence on the natural world. We live by inhaling the oxygen exhaled from trees and return the gift of life to them by exhaling the carbon dioxide that fuels their living. Worms burrow through the ground, aerating the soil so that plants can better take root and grow. Bees and wasps spend their lives flying from one flower to another, bringing life-giving pollination. The gift of nature is a laboratory teaching lessons of interdependence. The intricacies of ecological systems demonstrate the tenuous balance maintained when all parts function well and the devastation wrought when an ecosystem goes out of balance.

Scientists continue to warn about the disastrous effect of disregarding our connection with the natural world. Globally, production of crops like grain, a staple of our livelihood, are decreasing exponentially. Weather disruptions, likely associated with our carbon emissions, are causing extreme weather all over the globe, resulting in higher sea levels endangering all coastal cities, devastating heat waves destroying our crops and livestock, destructive wild fires and floods ravaging our communities, and hurricanes, typhoons and tornadoes randomly wreaking their devastation.

Unfortunately, our compartmentalized minds can allow us to hear all that information and remain in our human-centered bubble. Then a crisis happens close to home and with people we know. In Toledo, Ohio, just a few hours from where I live, toxins from algae on Lake Erie fouled the water supply, forcing officials to issue a warning to residents not to drink the water, brush their teeth, bathe or even shower. This water emergency went on for days, putting many lives at risk.

Where did the toxins come from? The phosphorous run-off from farm fertilizer and sewage treatment plants. Due to the increased demand for farm products, we increase production on our farms by using fertilizers. The same fertilizers that increase capacity for more production seep into the soil and eventually run off into our water supply, becoming a threat for the residents who ingest the toxins.

All of a sudden, the perilous effects of our casual disregard for the natural world came closer to home. When that happens, we cannot help but open our eyes to what has always been there but is now gone. And then, when it is nearly too late, we will realize we cannot continue to live for ourselves, denying the accumulating impact our choices make on the natural world. Our future and the future of God's created natural world are intimately bound together.

Recognizing our interconnectedness with the natural world is one step; taking responsibility for it is the next big step. When the psalmist says, "You have given them dominion over the works of your hands; you have put all things under their feet" (Ps 8:6), many assume God is giving us the right to dominate nature, to use it as if it were a slave to our desires, to exploit it and destroy it.

But *dominion* has a much different meaning. We are the only part of nature that can imagine the future and make intentional choices. So God gives to us the responsibility for the rest of creation—to love it, care for it and protect it. We exercise dominion over the creation as Jesus exercises dominion over our lives—through servant love.

As I sat in the rose garden in Pasadena I watched with renewed interest as the gardener pruned a few dead branches off the rose bush in front of me. Ironically, as he moved on to the next bed of flowers, I saw him bend over and pick up a plastic bottle someone had carelessly thrown into the grass. There it was. The paradox of our relationship with the natural world summed up in one moment.

ESSENTIAL LIFE QUESTION

How can I honor my interconnectedness with the natural world through the choices I make each day?

Practices

In the beginning, God created the cosmos, the earth, and all living and creeping things, and bound them together in a lyrical dance of interdependence. For all the ways we have fallen out of step with the natural world, we can begin by confessing our prideful self-centeredness. But then we must reengage the dance— stepping, twirling, delighting in and even tripping over our intimate partnership with the natural world—to rediscover the beauty that inspires, the connection that enlivens and the creative energy pulsing through all of it, for the sake of God's good world.

Notice. "Look at the birds of the air. . . . Consider the lilies of the field" (Mt 6:26, 28). The Creator of all that exists invites us to look, to consider. Our sensory connection with nature depends on where we live and the season of the year. So, make necessary adjustments based on where and when you do these practices. The guiding principle is that we cannot learn from nature unless we avail ourselves of the natural world, most often out of doors.

Find a spot—your "sit spot"—and go there every day, or as often as you can. While there, breathe deeply to center yourself in time and place and then become alert to your senses: What do you hear? What do you see? What do you smell? What can you touch, and how does it feel? Focus on something particular: a flower, a bird, a tree, an insect. Get to know it as you would a new friend. Just notice.

Notice what you notice. "But ask the animals, and they will teach you; the birds of the air, and they will tell you" (Job 12:7). During times of particular need or intentional discernment, take time to let God speak to you through nature. Our senses take in hundreds of thousands of impulses every minute, but our brains only notice a few—and for good reason. Those few are important. They mean something. Literally or metaphorically, they can speak to us a word we need to hear, a word that will inform our lives or a word that calls for response. Notice what you notice. Write it down. Ask of it, Why are you important? What can you teach me? Give a voice to whatever it is that you have noticed and let it speak back to you. Write down its words. This process can often move you into new understanding.

Act on what you have noticed. Sometimes what you have learned from what you notice will compel you to take action to change something in your personal life. Sometimes it will compel you to move into advocacy for the natural world. To find ways of taking this kind of action, do a web search for "organizations for the earth" or "care for the earth." There are likely groups in your community you can work with.

six

The Energy of Relationships

The storm clouds lifted. The journey of the past months had been treacherous at times, but little by little the sun's rays began breaking through. I had weathered the worst of it. Showers of confusion would still disrupt my life from time to time, but I no longer feared them. I even began to embrace them—the disruption they caused in life's routine, their necessity for growth and the nourishment they provided when my life felt parched. For the moment, I could live under the illusion that I was making progress.

Driving to see my spiritual director, I concluded that she had done her job. I was feeling better, more able to navigate the storms of life and more buoyant in spirit and outlook. I decided to tell her that this would be our last appointment. But as our conversation was drawing to a close, an alternate conversation began in my head.

Am I in relationship with people merely to get the job done? Do I use people to satisfy some need of mine and then when that need no longer exists or has subsided, the relationship no longer matters? Is that how I deal with all my relationships? A lengthy list of names of those who had moved in and out of my life scrolled through my mind. What is it about me that so easily releases relationships? What do I really believe about my need for other people, for community?

I began to think a parallel issue that I needed to struggle with, in addition to learning how to deal with life's storms, was how to experience the richness of everyday relationships, in stormy times and on sunny days. As I left, I set up another appointment. I still had work to do.

We, Not Me, in Creation

"So God created humankind in his image, in the image of God he created them; male and female he created them" (Gen 1:27). What an extraordinary assertion. All humans are made in the image of God. God's reflection emanates through individual lives and through community.

This assertion was exceedingly powerful for the Israelites during their time of exile. Surrounded by images of the Babylonian gods, they wondered how their God could be present, and they agonized over the thought that their God had been defeated, vanquished by a more powerful god, and excised from their lives. In response to their fears, the creation story asserted that God was still present, not in images made with hands, nor by brutal force of a conquering army, but in and through human life, human community.

In needed words of encouragement, God was present. In silent but knowing companionship, when the weight of grief seemed unbearable, God was present. In jokes and good humor that pierced the heaviness of their lives with levity and laughter, God was present. In a community that cared for widows, a family that nurtured children, a friend willing to make the journey with them, God was present.

Yet, was there more to this portion of the creation story than a gracious reminder of God's presence embedded in the exiled community? Consider this insight from Claus Westermann:

> God has created all people "to correspond to him," that is so that something can happen between creator and creature. This holds despite all differences among people; it goes beyond all differences of religion, beyond belief and unbelief. Every human being of every religion and in every place, even where religions are no longer recognized, has been created in the image of God.[1]

Westermann pushes us to expand our concept of the image of God. Through the act of creation, it is not just the faith community, the people of Israel and, by extension, you and I that reflect God's image. All people, created through the gracious design of God, reflect the image of their Creator: All people, not just the covenant people; all people, not just those we consider upright or palatable; all people, not just the ones that speak our language, support our causes, live in common neighborhoods or adopt common values. All people, created through the gracious design of God, reflect the image of their Creator.

Now, imagine what that idea might do for us as we consider what it means to live in a world immobilized by cultural suspicion, deadened by political backstabbing and posturing, fractured by religious strife and torn apart by warring states. Can God's grace release us from the misdirected desire to create life in our own image and open us to the possibility that God's image is present in us, in our communities and in all communities? Can we willingly confess not only our hesitancy but also our unwillingness to imagine *those* people, whoever *those* people are to us, as integral to God's grand design for human community? Will we allow ourselves to enter deeply into relationship with others, acknowledging our limitations and brokenness, and be open to having our horizons expanded by their presence as we together step into the flow of the renewable energy of relationships?

Do Deep

In her late thirties, my youngest sister decided to run a marathon. Though she was an athlete throughout high school and kept in relatively good shape chasing her three young kids, she was nowhere near marathon shape. Her husband, a veteran marathon runner, helped her design her training program. She gave herself ample time to prepare for the Memorial Day–

ESSENTIAL LIFE QUESTION

How does affirming that all people are created in the image of God affect how I see and treat them?

weekend race in Duluth, Minnesota. Still, there were two issues standing in her way. First, she would be training throughout the winter. This is not a big deal in many locations, but she lived in northern Minnesota. Second, she did not really love running. Subsequently, her husband described her race-day preparation with these words: "She didn't overtrain. She took the minimalist approach."

The path for Grandma's Marathon weaves along the shores of Lake Superior, ending in downtown Duluth, Minnesota. Eight miles into the marathon, my sister was feeling good, running at an acceptable pace, enjoying the scenery and already feeling a sense of accomplishment. She was a marathoner! Twelve miles in, her legs turned to cement blocks and she felt the building pressure of having to go to the bathroom. At mile eighteen she could not hold it any longer so she stopped, waited in line and went to the bathroom. Now, I am no marathon runner, but I imagine if you have followed a minimalist training regimen, run eighteen miles and then stopped for any length of time, restarting can be an issue. It was.

My sister staggered forward, legs cramping, running one minute and walking the next, running and walking, defeated. But as she closed in on the last few miles, the crowds started to gather along the raceway, fans wildly cheering and inspirational music playing. She talked about it as her Disney moment, the moment when supposedly you can dig deep and find a strength you did not know you had, which allows you to not just persevere but overcome and win!

As she told me later, "You know what, Kai? I found out I don't do deep!"

So she ran. Walked. Staggered. Stumbled. And finally crossed the line.

I don't do deep! Though it was her confession about a lack of physical strength for the race, I immediately extended the metaphor to our strength for the race of life, a strength derived from our relationships. How many of us take a minimalist, superficial approach to relationships? We don't do deep.

I learned a new phrase recently: "information grazers." Because of the preponderance of information available to us and our need to be perceived as competent in the eyes of others, we briefly scan reams of information, skimming what is pertinent off the top so we can seem conversant on any number of topics. We have become information grazers.

I wonder if we also have become relational grazers. We have more places to meet (clubs, malls, coffee shops, pubs, schools, workplaces, churches, homes) and more ways to connect (talk, text, Facebook, Instagram, Twitter, Skype), and yet we are lonelier than ever, more disconnected from one another and from ourselves. We don't do deep. Even when presented with the massive evidence that the depth of our relationships has a profound effect on who we are and the quality of our lives, we don't do deep.

Sociologists have studied the life-giving energy that comes through relationships. Tom Rath, in his book *Vital Friends*, documents the significance of friends for a full life. "Perhaps most importantly, strong social relationships are the leading indicator of our overall happiness, and these findings appear to hold up across countries and cultures."[2] Study after study on personal well-being points to the same conclusion: human beings thrive in human community.

The emerging field of brain studies intensifies the argument. Daniel Goleman, in his book *Social Intelligence*, reports that the scientific community has discovered that relationships wire us together, brain to brain. He writes, "Neuroscience has discovered that our brain's very design makes it sociable, inexorably drawn into an intimate brain-to-brain linkup whenever we engage with another person. That neural bridge lets us affect the brain—and so the body—of everyone we interact with, just as they do us."[3]

The sociological community and the scientific community affirm what faith communities have always known about the range of potential, life-changing benefits inherent in relationships. Yet we resist doing deep. Why? In my life and work, two primary reasons have surfaced: time and fear.

Time. It should be no surprise that hurried and harried living affects close relationships and the development of deeper relationships. When we buy into the accelerating pace of our society, we unwittingly put our relationships at risk. Love and deep friendships, including the emotional flexibility and creativity necessary to be in those relationships, only develop over time. John Ortberg articulates the consequence of a hurried life: "The most serious sign of hurry sickness is a diminished capacity to love. Love and hurry are fundamentally incompatible. Love always takes time, and time is one thing hurried people don't have."[4]

Relationships can only deepen over time through ordinary interactions filled with spontaneous laughter and knowing tears, conversations about ordinary events and complicated events. Beyond that, relationships thrive on surprising each other, cheering each other on, challenging each other to move forward and forgiving each other when we fail. Deep relationships take time.

Fear. Relationships thrive on vulnerability. But vulnerability taps into our fear: of ridicule, which prevents us from being open; of rejection, which prevents us from being honest; of betrayal, which prevents us from being trusting. One evening I walked through the family room as my kids were watching a documentary in which adult participants publicly shared their middle and high school diary entries. Exhilarating and excruciating. Painful and poignant. But what I found fascinating was how willing people were to share their deepest secrets and vulnerabilities—as if the participants were crying out for people to know who they were, and the audience was given implicit permission to later do the same.

How many relationships do we have where we are willing to be open about our joys and sorrows, our strengths and limitations, our triumphs and the times when we have given in to temptation? We live in a culture where image is everything, and by that I do not mean the image of God; I mean our image, the image we want people to see and admire. Social media has only exacerbated our ability to craft and perpetuate the image we want people to see.

In my own story, I now know that part of the pressure I was experiencing was the internal pressure to keep up my image. I did not want people to know my weaknesses, my fear of failing, so I created a cover, a false self that I believed was always insightful, always witty, always confident in my ability, for fear that I would be found out. Fear of rejection cuts off the life-enhancing energy of relationships.

Conversely, we may not fear being rejected in relationship as much as we fear being overwhelmed. What if the person needs more than we can or are willing to give? We have probably all entered relationships that at first seemed life giving, only to discover that our needs and the needs of the other did not match. It becomes quickly apparent that more personal, relational, even material resources will be required than we desire to give. Now we are trapped. We have become more to them than we wanted. Excising ourselves from those relationships comes at great cost.

> **ESSENTIAL LIFE QUESTION**
>
> What keeps me from desiring and therefore developing deeper relationships?

The Danger of a Single Story Line

We also fear people who are other, people who are different than we are. Chimamanda Ngozi Adichie is a Nigerian novelist and storyteller. In a TED talk titled "The Danger of a Single Story" she explores the pitfalls of being confined to a single story line.

When she was young, all the books she read were American or British children's books, thus they dealt with American or British themes. When she began to write stories at the age of seven she mirrored those themes in her writing, even though they had little connection to her real life and livelihood. All her characters were white skinned and blue eyed, though no one in her immediate community was white skinned or blue eyed. They all ate apples and drank ginger beer, though she had never eaten an apple or tasted ginger beer. Her characters routinely talked about the weather, especially when it snowed, though growing up in Nigeria, she had never experienced snow. For many years she wrote similar stories as those she had read, but never saw herself in them. It was as if she did not even exist in her own world of storytelling.

The stories we read and hear and experience have a powerful effect on how we envision the world and how we imagine our relationships with others. A single story line can keep us from seeing ourselves as part of the larger story, and it can also lead us to place unexamined judgment on people who are different from us and to demonize them.

Think about the implications for our culture with its ghettos and gated communities that isolate people in homogenous groups, its talk radio and cable television that demonize any divergent ideology, and religious institutions that cast judgment on all manner of people. Without consistent interaction with people from other walks of life we become insular, and our capacity to grow decreases. Single-story communities or families diminish the possibility that our minds will be altered or expanded in any way.

The insular Pharisaic community determined who was clean or unclean, in or out. No wonder they were so conflicted about this rabbi Jesus who dined with tax collectors and sinners, shared a water jug with a Samaritan woman, and touched and healed lepers. Their response? The leaders of the Pharisees questioned him under their breath (Lk 5:21), complained (Lk 5:30), watched him closely to bring charges against him (Lk 6:7), were infuriated (Lk 6:11), accused him of being a glutton and a drunk, a friend of tax collectors and sinners (Lk 7:34), were very hostile toward him (Lk 11:53), and even plotted to kill him (Lk 19:47).

They could not imagine, in fact, that they were threatened by another story line—a more expansive, more inclusive way of seeing God at work.

We have created a polarized world (racially, socioeconomically, politically, religiously). In this context, the hope for families, communities and nations rests on our desire and our capacity to move beyond a single story line. How can we both honor our unique story line and open ourselves to the story lines of others?

The contemporary context demands a new and concerted response to the neighbors in the world community, a response where we are less concerned about being right and more concerned about being in right relationship, less concerned about getting a point across and more concerned about crossing over the points that separate, less concerned about competition and more concerned about compassion. Can we reclaim who we are—image bearers of God—and re-envision others through that same lens? Are we willing to confess and release our deep-seated prejudice and fear in order to reconnect with one another, brothers and sisters created in the image of God? Can we start with our neighbors, our families and friends?

One of the most formative experiences I had in how to relate to others occurred when I stumbled over my own misguided enthusiasm. After attending an evangelism conference, I came home absolutely *on fire* for Jesus. You have to realize how strange this was for me, being both Norwegian (typically stoic and reserved) and Lutheran (typically formal and non-emotional). This was an out-of-body experience. The next evening I decided to abandon my prepared lesson plan for the Bible study I was teaching and set out to recruit a band of passionate evangelists for the cause. Fifteen minutes into the class, one of the students raised her hand and said, "Pastor, I am getting very uncomfortable with the tone of this study."

Taken aback, I said, "What is making you uncomfortable?"

She spoke candidly about her experience: "I am not a Christian. My sister invited me to this class because she said it would be a good way for me to explore what Christianity is all about. I liked the first few sessions, but this is making me feel very uncomfortable."

She paused, and fortunately I resisted a defensive reaction. She then continued,

> A friend of mine has been pestering me for months to attend her church. Each time she invites I decline, but she is relentless. A few weeks ago, I gave in and said I would attend an upcoming event. Wondering what that event was all about, I got on the church's website, clicked on the icon for the event and began to read. The opening line trumpeted that the event was going to be a perfect place to invite your unchurched friends. I started to feel trapped. What were they going to do once they got me there? So I called my friend and confronted her with a question. I needed her response before going any further. "Will you still be my friend if I never convert to Christianity?"

This question taught me more about sharing the gospel and about relationships than a three-day conference filled with high-powered, change-the-world lectures by pastors from some of the largest churches in the United States. Sharing the good news of Jesus' love for the world is all about relationships of mutual respect and long-term commitment, about love that is both broken and beautiful, muddling and moving, reluctant and restorative.

To follow Jesus is to open yourself to the renewing energy of relationships—all relationships—and simply honor them for what they are: gifts of God that mold and shape us with their pain and promise, everyday routine and spontaneous joy, regretful failure and renewing forgiveness. To the question "Will you still be my friend if I never convert to Christianity?" the answer must be "Yes!"

Practices

When God created humankind, God's image was reflected both in individual lives and in community. Both represent the goodness of God, the breadth of God's love and the source of God's power for creative life change. In a world divided by indifference and hatred, those willing to be bearers of the image will set their minds on making the journey together no matter the cost. There is no other option for image bearers of our creator God.

Single story line practice. Examining our formative story lines, we can discover both the linkages and disconnects they create in how we view others. In a journal or in conversation with family members or friends (if this would be helpful), respond to this question: When I was growing up, what are the stories I heard about other groups of people? Tell those stories, and examine the assumptions and prejudices they create. Then ask, What, if anything, has changed in how I view and/or interact with people in those groups? What would it mean for me to imagine them as created in the image of God, just as I am?

Daily walk. Take a daily walk with St. Francis using "The Prayer of St. Francis":

O Lord, make us instruments of Thy peace.
Where there is hatred, let us sow love;
Where there is injury, pardon;

Where there is doubt, faith;
Where there is despair, hope;
Where there is darkness, light;
Where there is sadness, joy;

O Divine Master, grant that we may not
so much seek to be consoled as to console;
to be understood as to understand;
to be loved as to love.

For it is in giving that we receive;
it is in pardoning that we are pardoned;
and it is in dying that we are born to eternal life.

As a daily exercise, take each phrase and make it the lens through which you see your relationships. For example, begin the day with the opening phrase, "O Lord, make us instruments of Thy peace." Throughout the day, repeat this phrase and look for ways to be an instrument of peace. At the end of the day reflect on the opportunities to serve others in this unique way. Focus on a single phrase for as many days as you choose. When you wish to move on, take the next phrase, "Where there is hatred, let us sow love," and repeat the process.

seven

The Energy of
Fruitful Work

Y ou're back!" a parishioner remarked after one of my sermons. Not having traveled anywhere in many months, I found it a curious statement, so I followed up. "What do you mean?"

"There is just something settled about you," she said. "You're less anxious and more joyful."

She was right. I was in the same city, the same job, the same relationships, but I had embarked on a significant journey leading me to a new place. Her comment sent me on a quest to figure out what it was specifically that constituted this new place.

God's grace had released me from my unrealistic expectations and the burdensome expectations of community members. All I could do was live the life I had been given, open myself to God's renewing spirit, do my best and trust that is enough. I also had come to a place in my spirit where, if that was not good enough for the people I served, I was free to move on. While I did not desire or plan to move, I was free to move on if they needed me to be something that I could not be.

That freedom unlocked the energy of possibility. To give my

best to this place, I needed to spend a majority of my time doing work that enlivened me: teaching, working individually with others, inspiring the people of God to live more meaningful lives and joyfully cherishing the gift of everyday life. Living out of my strengths energized me and, I trusted, would energize others. I was rediscovering the renewable energy of fruitful work.

I was back.

The Blessing of Fruitful Work

"God blessed them, and God said to them, 'Be fruitful and multiply'" (Gen 1:28). Having been created in God's image, humankind received God's blessing and the command to be fruitful and multiply. Traditionally this command has been connected to the capacity to procreate and populate the earth. There is, however, another dimension to be considered. To bear fruit and multiply can also mean that we are meant to reproduce God's goodness and blessing in our lives for the sake of the world.

Claus Westermann writes, "The power and dynamism of the blessing enables people to 'fill the earth and subdue it,' and to make, discover, and invent. The blessing penetrates far more deeply into the story of humanity; the creator does not bestow ready-made products on people, but gives them the capacity to acquire and to create."[1] God created us to offer ourselves and our creativity to the world through our paid work, our volunteering and the tasks of everyday life. The Hebrew word for work (*abad*) means to serve.[2] Fruitful work infuses energy into people's lives, connecting who they are with the ways they can uniquely serve in the world.

One of the life-giving ministries in the congregation I serve is our ministry to disabled adults. We host twenty to thirty guests from area group homes one night a week for Bible study and singing, one Saturday a month as a day of respite for their caregivers, and one week a year for an onsite camping experience. As you can imagine, not everyone feels equipped for this ministry, but for those who open their hearts and make the investment of time and energy, there are few experiences of comparable delight and joy.

As I was watching the campers arrive for this year's camp, I was struck by one of our volunteers—the joy on her face, the love she extended. As her camp companion arrived, she placed her hands gently on either side of the camper's face and said, "I am so glad to see you again this year. You look beautiful." The joy was palpable. The sheer delight of the moment overwhelmed me.

After everyone had gathered, I pulled this volunteer aside and told her how extraordinary her response was to her camper. Her words struck me. "I was so frightened to go to the nightly Bible study a few years ago. I didn't know if I had what it takes to serve in this ministry. But now I've found what I'm here for!"

As I walked down the hallway, I imagined what it would have been like for the campers and this volunteer if she had let fear overtake her and cause her to hide her talent. The joy would never have been experienced. The love would never have been expressed. "I've found what I'm here for." That is the renewable energy of fruitful work.

ESSENTIAL LIFE QUESTION
What am I here for at this time?

When Jesus speaks about bearing fruit, he connects it with both the outward manifestation of love and the inner experience of joy: "I have said these things to you so that my joy may be in you, and that your joy may be complete. This is my commandment, that you love one another as I have loved you" (Jn 15:11-12). Fruitful work in the workplace, neighborhood, community and at home always leans outward in love. In this case, love is not just sentiment or good feelings; love manifests itself in very concrete ways. Society needs honest people of good integrity in politics leading nations, in homes nurturing children, in communities organizing acts of justice, in schools inspiring students.

Fruitful work manifests itself in specific acts of love wherever we find ourselves. The energy of fruitful work also gives us an inner motivation that spurs us on, even in challenging times. Over the years, I have been struck by the number of thought leaders across many disciplines who have variously described this inward drive. One of my favorite thinkers, Mihaly Csikszentmihalyi, writes about the concept of flow. He describes flow as "the state in which people are so involved in an activity that nothing else seems to matter; the experience itself is so enjoyable that people will do it at great cost, for the sheer sake of doing it."[3]

Even without using the language of faith, Csikszentmihalyi taps into the deep wisdom of God embedded in the story of creation. When we engage in fruitful work, we discover the wellspring of God's energy flowing through us, increasing both our capacity for the task at hand and our resilience in the face of obstacles. That is why we are here.

Jesus speaks about this inner experience, this inner motivation, as joy: "I have said these things to you so that my joy may be in you, and that your joy may be complete" (Jn 15:11). For Jesus, joy is not the superficial happiness that so many in our culture seek—happiness almost completely dependent on external circumstances. It is the abiding satisfaction of knowing that we are God's people no matter what, created to extend the fruits of God's love in the world.

ESSENTIAL LIFE QUESTION

What in my life brings me joy?

The Fruit of Fruitful Work

You might ask, How do I know if I am experiencing or expressing the renewable energy of fruitful work? Though there are no hard and fast definitions for fruitful work, the short answer is this: whenever and wherever goodness and love flow into the world, fruitful work is being done. Since fruitful work is a gift of God, our fruitful work will reflect God's nature and character, God's kindness and love, God's justice and mercy. Here are four fruits of our fruitful work.

No distinctions. I have always admired my sister Linnea. She is bright, engaging, proactive in work and life, and deeply connected to the energy of God. It shows. I remember the first time my wife and I visited her in her executive role at a prestigious East Coast hospital. As we toured the facility, people on all levels—parking lot attendants and professional health care providers, janitors and hospital administrators—stopped what they were doing, smiled and greeted her. "Linnea, good to see you today." She, in turn, called each by name and introduced them to us like they were the most important people at the hospital. There was no distinction. When we are engaged in the fruitful work of God we will reflect God's nature, relating to all with the same intentionality and love.

People over procedure. Think about these responses to acts of service: "I was more than a number to them." "They didn't look at me as a problem but as a person." "When I was with them, it seemed like I was the only person that mattered in that moment." What is the common link? People engaging in fruitful work recognize and honor the human dignity of others.

We all know what it is like when we are dismissed or overlooked, when our worth is valued only for what we purchase or the potential gain we represent. We become resentful and wonder why we ever engaged that relationship, whether in a coffee shop or the next cubicle, volunteering at school or the local food pantry. Conversely, we know what it is like when someone respects who we are, when we are treated with dignity. It makes all the difference.

Periodically, when my wife and I are out in the community, a person I do not know stops us and gushes about how important my wife was to them after they had their baby. My wife works with new moms, specifically helping them with breastfeeding issues. As she says, "There are technical things I can do to help moms with the process of breastfeeding, but my work usually consists of helping them deal with the emotional issues surrounding being a new mom." What the new moms tell me, after they enthusiastically show my wife all the pictures of their growing child, is not how good my wife was as a technician (though she is), but how my wife cared for them through this unexpectedly precarious journey of new motherhood. When we fully participate in the fruitful work we have been given, people will always take precedence over procedures.

Extra mile. For those participating in the fruitful work God has given them to do, there will always be a sense of, and a capacity for, going the extra mile, even when it is hard. Over the years, I have been impressed with so many teachers and school administrators who chose to look at the whole circumstance of their students' lives, not simply what happens during school hours. "This student's family is going through a difficult job transition and money is tight. Can we find a way to provide school supplies?" "This student's parents are divorcing. Can we work together to provide some counseling?" "This student's family just arrived from another country and they have very little to establish a new home. Can we help them in the transition?"

Fruitful work is a way of life, not an action on our to-do list. Those who are energized by their fruitful work find the capacity to go the extra mile.

Humility. Those who understand the nature of fruitful work know that ultimately the work is not about them. You know what it is like when the prideful attitude of people offering themselves in service overtakes the work they do. Whether it is through specific words or a pompous posture, their focus is, Look what I have done! Their arrogance diminishes their action.

You have probably also experienced the beauty of humble servanthood when fruitful work gets done with little regard for personal recognition or acclaim. (I say "little" rather than "no" because there are few of us, if any, who are ever purely altruistic in our motives.) It feels more authentic, more of God. All who are involved are infused with greater energy for the work at hand.

Now, I would like you to notice this: Each of these fruits is radically countercultural. In a divisive, prideful, production-oriented culture, the fruits of unity and respect, sacrifice and humility offer an alternate vision of what the world can be. In the end, God longs not simply for us to make a difference in the world but for the world to be different—more reflective of God's nature and intent, more loving, compassionate, inclusive, hopeful.

I have often called this a quiet revolution of love. No flashing billboards. No mass media blitzes. Just people like you and me, offering our flawed selves to a broken world, trusting that God's life and energy can live through us, each ordinary day, each un-momentous moment.

The Money Issue

In God's economy, parents nurturing and challenging their children to discover their uniqueness are doing fruitful work in the same way as the president of a nation working faithfully to create peace and build networks of advocacy and justice is doing fruitful work. A thoughtful teacher on Main Street and a philanthropic investor on Wall Street both have a place in God's economy.

In God's economy every expression of fruitful work is of value. However, in the human economy these jobs are rewarded very differently. This can cause both internal and external conflict.

My grandfather was the only one of thirteen children to emigrate from Norway to the United States. He came with nothing but an eighth grade education. First he worked on the Great Lakes ships, then as a taxi driver, then as a day laborer on construction sites. He finally worked his way up to vice president of a small construction company. He provided well enough for his family, but in his mind it was never enough. In addition, he had the immigrant mentality of wanting his son to do better. When my father, after a teenage conversion, announced that he was considering a career in the ministry, my grandfather responded, "You're a fool! You'll never make a dime." It was clear what drove my grandfather's decision making.

So, what will drive your decisions?

Because income provides material gain and power and prestige, it is difficult not to resent the pervasive inequities in pay. Foul-mouthed entertainers can earn millions of dollars spewing their venom while soft-spoken hospice workers, compassionately ushering our loved ones over the threshold between life and death, can barely earn enough to provide for their family of four. A parent who chooses to stay at home and do the difficult work of raising children earns nothing at all. To honestly be open to the energy of fruitful work, we must make peace with the almighty dollar, because money, power and the accumulation of possessions can blur the motivation for life's work.

An article in *The Atlantic* reveals the conflict we experience in our culture. Parents were asked whether they focus on empathy or achievement more as they raise their children. Overwhelmingly, they said that empathy was their primary focus. When their children were asked what was most important for their parents and the focus of their parenting, the overwhelming response was achievement. The authors of the study note, "While 96 percent of parents say they want to raise ethical, caring children, and cite the development of moral character as 'very important, if not essential,' 80 percent of the youths surveyed reported that their parents 'are more concerned about achievement or happiness than caring for others.'"[4] We say one thing, but our actions reveal the truth.

Though we might be conflicted about it, achievement, money and prestige are described with great clarity throughout the Scriptures as a seductive trap. In the Sermon on the Mount, Jesus speaks about the tension inherent in living in the world: "Do not store up for yourselves treasures on earth. . . . For where your treasure is, there your heart will be also. . . . No one can serve two masters. . . . You cannot serve God and wealth" (Mt 6:19-24). In Luke 12, Jesus teaches the crowds: "Be on your guard against all kinds of greed; for one's life does not consist in the abundance of possessions." He then goes on to tell the story of a man who built many barns to house his ever-increasing, bountiful harvest but ended up losing his soul (Lk 12:15-21).

Throughout the Bible, there were people of great wealth, but with wealth came greater responsibility. Paul writes, "As for those who in the present age are rich, command them not to be haughty, or to set their hopes on the uncertainty of riches, but rather on God who richly provides us with everything for our enjoyment. They are to do good, to be rich in good works, generous, and ready to share" (1 Tim 6:17-18).

It is also clear in the Bible that money itself is not the issue; rather, the problem is the passion it arouses in us. We see people who haven't worked as hard as we have and yet have more, and we become resentful. Or we see people who have less than we have, and we become judgmental. We think about how little we have been able to save and we become fearful that it will not be enough, or we look at what we have been able to accumulate and we feel pride. We see all that money can buy and we want more, more, more, or we hoard what we have and are unable to share.

The seduction of wealth has been a consistent theme for followers of Jesus throughout the centuries. It is apparent that this is a significant issue in contemporary decision making as well. Though a reasonable income can be a consideration in the pursuit of fruitful work, it cannot be the only consideration.

ESSENTIAL LIFE QUESTION

What role does money—the accumulating of it and the spending of it—play in my sense of identity, my relationships, my use of time, my way of life?

What Next?

One of the deceptive thoughts in contemporary life is that God has a perfect place for us to serve where all our gifts will be used to the fullest, we will never be bored, and we will get along with one another perfectly. We assume our task is to find that job or volunteer opportunity, that utopian place of fruitful work, in order to find contentment.

Dallas Willard dispels that notion in his book *Hearing God*. Willard begins by quoting Gary Friesen: "The major point is this: God does not have an ideal, detailed life-plan uniquely designed for each believer that must be discovered in order to make correct decisions." Willard then responds, "So the perfect will of God may allow, for a particular person, a number of different alternatives."[5]

Still, many people find themselves trapped in a job or a place in life that neither gives them energy nor nurtures them in healthy ways. Some discover later in life that the path they chose has little connection to the person they have become. Some choose simply to ride it out and wait until they retire to live fully. Others live in a state of perpetual denial, gobbling up as much life as they can now and living for the moment.

For many, this existential dilemma pierces them to the soul and often isolates them in their questions. They long for something else, but they feel imprisoned in their established life. They are quick to say, "If only I would have done this, studied that, listened to my heart way back when, I'm sure I would be much happier now!" Or their despair does not reflect opportunities lost but rather lack of opportunities at all.

This process of life reflection and discernment needs to be handled with great care. Flogging ourselves for past decisions or past circumstances can become a never-ending cycle of resentment, paralyzing us from moving forward. On the other hand, abrupt life changes can be equally destructive.

If the decision to change location, job, relationships is made precipitously, without regard to who you are, to what is life giving, to the needs of your family, but is done to escape a given situation, it can simply be a way to avoid the deeper life questions you are struggling with. In that case, you bring the same internal discontent to any new place, new role or new relationship.

It may be helpful to adopt a long view of the situation we are in rather than seeking to flee quickly from the smothering discontent. That may not mean finding another job or position in life; instead, it may mean reframing our current state of life, recasting our job, reinvesting time in life-giving relationships, or re-envisioning what can be done with time outside of work. At certain phases in life, it may be enough to discover a place to volunteer that satisfies a need to give while still providing resources to live reasonably in the world. It may also be the impetus to evaluate assumptions about what is truly needed in one's life.

Recall the words of the Serenity Prayer from a previous chapter: "God grant me the serenity to accept the things I cannot change; the courage to change the things I can; and the wisdom to know the difference." Navigating these transitions requires acceptance of decisions made in the past (even the ones you regret), courage to honestly face your present circumstance and risk moving forward, and a deep and abiding wisdom that discerns appropriate timing and anticipated impact on relationships.

Practices

To be led to that place of fruitful work we must be open to, listen to and be willing to follow the nudging of the Spirit. We may not know exactly where the Spirit will lead, but as we find ourselves in a place where we can offer love to neighbors, coworkers and the community and experience even a fleeting sense of joy, chances are we are on the way.

There are two practices to consider. The first helps us reframe our daily living and work. The second invites us to reflect on our relationship with money.

Love and joy. Through the lens of love and joy, examine each part of your daily life and ask these questions: How can I share more of God's love in this place? How can I experience more joy in this place?

Relationship with money. Over two hundred biblical texts reference money or wealth. There are a number of perspectives about money found in the Bible. As you read through some of these texts, think about which perspectives most reflect your thinking about money.

- *Money is a reward:* We have because we have earned and God has rewarded (Gen 24:34-35).

- *Money is a right for all:* The early Christians sold all they had and shared their resources. Everyone had enough (Acts 2:44-47; 4:32-37).

- *Money is a gift:* God blesses some with great wealth. They neither earn nor deserve it but only must receive it. Does not God clothe the lilies of the field (Mt 6:28-30)?

- *The lack of money is a gift:* "Blessed are you who are poor" (Lk 6:20).

- *Money is a curse:* Wealth has a seductive power, and those who have it or want it are easily corrupted. We have an insatiable need for more and have therefore lost our freedom (Mt 6:19-21).

How does this way of thinking affect, for good or for ill, your attitude toward your life and your possessions, toward others with more than you and others with less than you?

eight

The Energy of Rest

The end of an intense ministry season coincided with the final weeks of a school year and the frenetic pace of concerts, sports, tests and homework for our four kids. For weeks there was little or no margin in our schedules. Times together with my wife were like logistics meetings for a taxi service, charting who was going to be where, when, and how many open seats would be needed in the cars. During that time, I reminded myself that relief was on the way by chanting this daily mantra: *Twenty more days until vacation. Nineteen more days until vacation . . .*

Preparing for vacation on Bald Head Island added stress to the days immediately preceding our departure: shopping for travel needs, finding people to cover my job at church, packing our suitcases and arranging for our house to be cared for while we were gone. I remember thinking, *There are not enough days on the island to fully decompress.*

After two days of travel, we arrived at the ferry landing and unpacked what seemed like a month's worth of luggage for our five-day stay. Then we parked the car, loaded our family on the ferry and separated from the mainland.

The pace of the first few days seemed like the pace we had just left, though the change in environment itself had carved out some space in my soul. The third day on the beach welcomed me to that place my body and spirit craved, the place of rest. After an hour of crashing in the waves, I sank into my beach chair, novel in hand, and prepared for an afternoon of immersion in another world. Not more than five minutes into my reading, my eyes drooping, my head bobbing and the book intermittently falling from my hands due to my drowsiness, I gave in to my body's call and laid down on a beach towel under the umbrella, closed my eyes and checked out of the world. A few minutes of shut-eye turned to an hour or more as my body sank into the sand and my breathing became one with the gentle rhythm of the incoming tide. At last my body was open to receive the creative energy and renewal of rest.

The Rhythm of Work and Rest

"Thus the heavens and the earth were finished, and all their multitude. And on the seventh day God finished the work that he had done, and he rested on the seventh day from all the work that he had done. So God blessed the seventh day and hallowed it, because on it God rested from all the work that he had done in creation" (Gen 2:1-3). From the beginning, the faith community has confessed that the essential rhythm of life swings between full engagement and intentional disengagement, between times of creating and re-creating, between times of hard work and restorative rest. In ancient Israel, a day was set aside to honor the God who gave life and the ability to work and produce, a day to participate in God's life by stopping, like God did on the seventh day, and enjoying the fruits of work.

The giving of the covenant law through Moses on Mount Sinai codified the sabbath as a day of rest: "Remember the sabbath day, and keep it holy. Six days you shall labor and do all your work. But the seventh day is a sabbath to the LORD your God; you shall not do any work—you, your son or your daughter, your male or female slave, your livestock, or the alien resident in your towns" (Ex 20:8-10). In Leviticus 25, the sabbath rhythm is connected with the land itself: "Six years you shall sow your field, and six years you shall prune your vineyard, and gather in their yield; but in the seventh year there shall be a sabbath of complete rest for the land, a sabbath for the LORD: you shall not sow your field or prune your vineyard" (Lev 25:3-4). What is true for humans is true for all of creation: rest restores.

Claus Westermann refers to the unique blessing of the sabbath in the community of faith. It "gives the day, which is a day of rest, the power to stimulate, animate, enrich, and give fullness to life. It is not the day in itself that is blessed, but rather the day in its significance for the community."[1]

Observance of the sabbath became a sign of identity for the people of Israel in the midst of competing religious traditions and foreign cultures. Who were those people refraining from work one day a week? The people of Israel. Why would they persist in such an unproductive rhythm, why defy the norms of the dominant cultures? Because the sabbath was a weekly reminder that the people of Israel were not in ultimate control, God was. They could stop for that day, rest and enjoy the pleasure of one another and the gifts that God gave them while the world continued even without their efforts.

The sabbath invites us to trust that God will provide, that the world does not depend on constant work to continue and that our ultimate worth does not come through achievements but through God's grace and love. To live a sabbath life we must struggle with the tension of living in a culture that puts its trust in busyness as a badge of honor rather than restoration as a building block for our humanity; puts its confidence in our ability to produce rather than God's desire to provide for us; pins its hopes on striving for achievement of greatness rather than soaking in God's affirmation of grace.

Imagine this: how outrageous would it be if our identity as a community of faith was shaped by sabbath and someday people would say of us, *Why are those people choosing not to work so much? Why aren't they more driven to out-produce everyone else?* *Why don't they buy in to the prevailing cultural norms of achievement and affirmation? What is with them?* If that is what they see in us, they will have observed the renewable energy of rest.

ESSENTIAL LIFE QUESTION
What does renewing rest look like for me?

A Daily Sabbath Rhythm

The sabbath is not just a day. It is a way of being, a rhythm that honors the Creator and energizes life. A sabbath rhythm for a day connects us biblically with the daily provision of manna that God provided the people of Israel as they wandered in the wilderness (Ex 16:4) and the prayer for daily bread at the center of the Lord's Prayer (Lk 11:3). The longing for daily renewal and God's promise of daily sustenance for bodies and souls come together in this daily sabbath rhythm.

A sabbath rhythm, though not easy in our contemporary world, is an essential task in order to celebrate the gift of the day, the fruitful work we have been given and the gracious presence of a God whom we can trust. The bad news is that the constant noise, distraction and seduction of more in our culture fuels discontented spirits. The good news is that we have choices. We can say no, turn off the constant white noise of television, take out the ear buds, shut down tablets and computers, set aside our smartphones and quiet ourselves before God. But it takes conscious and intentional work.

One necessary piece of work involves dismantling the cultural virtue of multitasking. In a world rapidly increasing in the amount and the pace of information production and assimilation, multitasking, like busyness, has become a badge of honor and a résumé booster for workers in the twenty-first-century marketplace. But what we are learning—sometimes the hard way through the upswing in stress-related illnesses and lower productivity in the workplace—is that our brains were not made for multitasking.

Harvard professor Daniel Goleman dispels the myth: "Then there's what many people think of as 'splitting' attention in multi-tasking, which cognitive science tells us is a fiction, too. Rather than having a stretchable balloon of attention to deploy in tandem, we have a narrow, fixed pipeline to allot. Instead of splitting it, we actually switch rapidly. Continual switching saps attention from full, concentrated engagement."[2]

A constant bombardment of competing information is counterproductive for our work, and it saps our energy and creativity. Rather, a rhythm of active engagement and retreat allows us to focus on the task at hand, as well as giving our brain the open space it needs to do creative work. For those who have greater ability to manage their schedules, it could mean creating space in between appointments or setting aside specific time during the day for email or phone messages rather than feeling obligated to respond to them at all times. For others whose schedules are set, deliberately using break times or lunch times to walk or have enjoyable conversation or read something stimulating rather than working through your breaks can give your mind its

needed respite. For parents, it may mean avoiding the temptation to overschedule your kids' activities and instead intentionally create more space for free play.

The same is true for our intentional lives of faith. When we
create a sabbath rhythm for our days we intentionally set aside
time to rest, to be quiet before God, to focus, to listen. There are
a number of spiritual practices that can usher in a time for rest,
but one of the most significant, especially for those caught in the
tyranny of busyness, is solitude. Richard Foster, in his book *Prayer*,
writes, "In solitude we voluntarily abstain from our normal patterns of activity and interaction with people for a time in order to
discover that our strength and well-being come from God alone."[3]

Solitude takes us to a quiet center where we can release all of
the things in life that prop us up: our pursuit of recognition or
achievement, our state of perpetual motion and the emotional
scaffolding of relationships that keeps us from addressing our
own issues. In that way, there is both promise and peril inherent
in making solitude a consistent part of life. Foster writes, "Pain-
fully, we let go of the vain images of ourselves in charge of
everything and everybody. Slowly, we loosen our grip on all those
projects that to us seem so significant. Gently, we become more
focused and simplified. Joyfully, we receive the nourishment of
heavenly manna."[4] Regretfully, many avoid times of quiet and
solitude because they do not want to admit what is going on in
their lives. They avoid listening to their lives fearing they will
hear nothing but disappointment and failure.

What I have learned from my own journey is this: the reason
I ran from God is, in fact, the best reason to run toward God.
When gripped by regret, when drenched in disappointment and
when confronted by failure, I felt my energy drain out of me. In
solitude, on the other hand, the Spirit of God releases, then

transforms, the power that regret, disappointment and failure have over life and infuses a new power and vitality for life. The apostle Paul experienced this life-giving gift when he received these words: "My grace is sufficient for you, for power is made perfect in weakness" (2 Cor 12:9).

Solitude creates the space in our busy lives for the Spirit to speak, announcing healing for wounded spirits, encouragement for faint hearts, peace for fearful lives and new strength for active service. As we engage in solitude, we may have the distinct feeling that nothing is going on because we do not sense anything happening. But these less than scintillating times of solitude can also be instructive. Remember, these practices are not magic treatments that realign spiritual physiology to alleviate symptoms. Just as it is sometimes enough to simply be with someone you love, not saying a word but being fully present, it is also enough to be alone with God, not saying or hearing a word but simply resting in God's presence.

As an extroverted, relational person, the practice of solitude seemed not only foreign but painful. One of my great discoveries was the renewing energy of rest I experienced through small daily practices of solitude. The first barrier I had to overcome was the all-or-nothing barrier. If I could not do a half hour or more, I would not do anything at all. In starting to practice solitude (and by that I mean sitting alone quietly in my office with the door closed doing nothing) five minutes at a time, then ten, I discovered the power of consistent, short sabbath moments. During this time, my breathing slowed. My shoulders dropped. My mind cleared. I rested. The issues I had before that time were still present when I re-entered my workspace. But I did so with renewed energy.

Matters of time are often a critical issue for most of us. I have often heard myself and others saying, "I don't have time to get everything done." "How can I add one more thing?" Maybe the question we need to ask is, Can we rethink what we are already doing and reimagine it as an opportunity for sabbath rest?

An attorney in the congregation I serve decided to shut off her car radio on her way to and from work. Instead of filling her head with more noise, she used that twenty to thirty minutes to think and pray about her job on the way to work and her family on the drive home.

One person, wrestling with significant job and family transitions, posted the words "Jesus loves me, no matter what" on his bathroom mirror, his computer screen, his phone and everywhere else he would look during the day. Each time he saw the words, he would pause, say a brief prayer and remember that prevailing love.

I, like so many others, seem to live by the prompting of reminders on my phone. Knowing that, I have built a habit of consistent quiet by scheduling prayer reminders on my phone three times a day. Each time my appointment reminder says, "Love's reach" (one of our worship themes), I pause and ask myself, *In what part of my life do I need to receive love? To whom can I extend love?*

Another friend, a mom of two extremely active kids, decided to use her time of walking the dog in the morning to sing praise songs and pray. Her only obstacle was her neighbor's peculiar response to the crazy lady walking up and down the street talking to herself. A good friend and pastoral colleague takes this one step further, writing a periodic blog titled "A Spirituality of Dog Walking," where he documents his thoughts and insights that come while walking his dog.

Can you reimagine what you are already doing as an opportunity for daily sabbath rest and renewal?

A Weekly Sabbath Rhythm

When I was growing up in Morris, Minnesota, in the 1970s, blue laws restricted retail shops from being open on Sunday. Talk about a relic of a longed-for past! Those days are gone. Not only are there few days in a year when shopping malls are closed, but the preponderance of sports and dance and music activities scheduled for kids have encroached on every day of the week, every hour of the day.

Anyone who attempts a weekly sabbath rhythm faces tremendous hurdles. For many, the sabbath (Friday evening to Saturday evening for Jews and Sunday for Christians) has become a time to catch up on work rather than a time to refrain from work. The insanity of weekly schedules leaves little time for the mundane and necessary chores of maintaining a home. So even if individuals do pause for an hour or so for worship, the sabbath becomes time to finish anything undone so that they can enter into the insanity of the week on Monday morning.

Claiming a consistent rhythm of weekly sabbath takes at least as much intentionality and creativity as it takes to carve out time for solitude or daily sabbath. The process begins by asking ourselves key questions: *What activities renew my body, my soul, my relationships? Before I say yes to anything else, when will I do those things? What activities deaden my soul? Are they truly necessary?*

By asking those questions, our weekly sabbath can stand in stark contrast to our culture of perpetual motion and reorient us to those things that make us most alive. That is why worship became so central to the weekly rhythm of the faith community. During worship, followers of Jesus remind themselves of and offer themselves to the God who makes all things new, who gives the gift of rest.

Worship reorients our hearts around the essential questions of life so that we are not just responding to the ordinary questions of every day. Being part of a worshiping community allows us to step out of the torrid pace of life, with its insidious pressure to produce and achieve, and reconnect with the source of life and vitality through God's Spirit and the presence of others on a common journey. A worshiping community reminds us we are not alone.

Given the frantic pace set by many, the very act of getting to worship can cause more anxiety than it seems it is worth. Candidly, on some days, it may be worth it to stay home. Periodically my wife tells our kids to stay in their pajamas, that it is enough for us to be together, to rest, to enjoy. On those days the creative energy of grace and the creative energy of rest dance together.

On the other hand, the effort that it takes to get to worship can also be seen as the upfront work we do to welcome a guest into our home. Once the work is done, the lights dimmed and the guests have arrived, we can relax into an evening of eating wonderful food, hearing interesting stories and enjoying being together. Similarly, it takes effort to get to church. But once we get there, we can relax into the beauty of the music, be edified by the sermon and celebrate our connection to the community.

Weekly sabbath can also include attention to relationships that renew the spirit, recreation that strengthens the body and activities that uniquely nurture your soul. The primary question for weekly sabbath is, what activity will help you reorient and restore your mind or rest and renew your body? All of us will need to answer that question for ourselves.

For some it may mean setting aside time to get the house back in order so that you can breathe more easily as you engage your week. For others, a weekly date with family or friends helps ground you in what is most important. For still others, a physical excursion that you did not have time for during the week sets your body, and thus your mind, back in a good space. As you know, these times will not just happen on their own. Tapping into the wellspring of God's energy through times of rest requires intentional fore-thought and a conscious desire to open space in your calendar and a place in your heart for God's Spirit to renew your life.

A Sabbath Rhythm for Life

The rhythm of sabbath rest and renewal breathes life into our daily and weekly rhythms when we intentionally set aside time to be filled with the energy of God. But sabbath is more than just a way of setting aside time; it is a way of life. Notice the pattern of Jesus' life as he moves between times of active engagement and intentional disengagement. In Luke's Gospel, Jesus withdraws to pray eight times (Lk 4:42; 5:16; 6:12; 9:18, 28; 11:1; 21:37; 22:41). He seems to know instinctively when his body and soul need to be renewed. He incorporates a sabbath rhythm into his life.

One of the scenes is particularly instructive. In Luke 4:42, the crowds, craving the healing power of Jesus, search him out after he withdraws to pray. When they find him, the text says, "they wanted to prevent him from leaving them." But in spite of their wishes, Jesus moves on and withdraws from the crowds, though there is much work to be done, many people to be healed. Even when they come clawing and clutching after him, begging him to stay, he knows what he is called to do and moves on. Jesus had limits to his energy. Why would we ever assume that we do not?

Getting in touch with a sabbath rhythm for life allows us to know when we need to refuel. Exhaustion causes anger and frus-tration in the human spirit, and busyness in life can strain rela-tionships. Those who consciously adapt a sabbath rhythm for life know when they need to withdraw or find time to renew. My wife's father used to say, "The car runs just as well on the top half of the gas tank as it does on the bottom half," as he tried to teach his daughters to watch the gas gauge. Our lives run better when we learn to refuel before getting to a critical point of depletion.

Over time, a sabbath rhythm will include times of vacation. In the short term, it might mean taking a half day off when needed, going on a long walk to clear the head, working in the yard, reconnecting with an old friend for an encouraging conversation or finding time to be intimate with your loved one. Those who open themselves to the renewing energy of rest and experiment with different practices soon learn what works and what does not. Then they are able to make choices.

ESSENTIAL LIFE QUESTION

What might I intentionally do to renew my body, my mind and my spirit?

Practices

Jürgen Moltmann writes, "The pulse of life is found in the rhythms of the times and in the alternation between work and rest."[5] In a double-shot-of-espresso culture, juiced by five-hour energy and monster drinks, we come to distrust the renewing, energizing power of God's Spirit. We do not want to wait for God; we want to create on our own. Yet God has woven a rhythm for life into the fabric of the cosmos. When life is revitalized, fruitfulness follows. And the universe sings a song of praise to its Creator for the renewable energy of rest.

Solitude. Since each person's normal routine and personal needs are different, it is difficult to prescribe a specific way to enter into a time of solitude. But here are a few suggestions to experience the renewing energy of this gift on a daily basis.

- Find a consistent time. Start with just a few minutes and increase the time as you get more comfortable with solitude.

- Find a place away. If you are a nature person, sit outside or inside where you can notice the beauty of creation. Create a quiet space in your home. Shut the door to your office. If you have important symbols or pictures or images that connect you with God, place them around you.

- Breathe deeply for a period of time, centering yourself in that moment, that space. Know that God's Spirit is present.

- After centering, pay attention to thoughts or impressions or names of people that come to mind. Some will just be the mind wandering, so release those. Others might make you wonder. Note them in some way. Then return to your time of quiet. If nothing noteworthy comes, just be glad that you had time to quiet yourself. That time alone is important for your body, your mind and your spirit.

- As you reenter your world, reflect on those things you noted and ask, Is this something I need to follow up on? What steps do I need to take? Then, reengage your world with new power and insight.

"More essential things" plan. In the introduction I mentioned the "More Everything" plan from my wireless carrier. Rather than a "more everything" plan, you can create your own "more essential things" plan.

Write down the activities that are life giving for you. Then do an audit of all the things in your life that create extra noise or confusion or just fill time. Which ones are necessary? Which ones can be left behind? Try, for a day at a time and then a week, not to do those things. Instead, use some of that time just to be quiet or to do something from your list that gives you life. For example, can you turn your radio or CD player off on the way to work and travel in silence? Can you do a TV fast for a period of time and use that time for yourself or to be with your family or friends? Can you take a walk alone during a work break? What would a "more essential things" plan look like for you? Write it down.

Conclusion

Trusting the Slow
Work of God

It has been a few years since my unwanted gift forced me to question myself, my image of God and my place in the world. From the perspective of time, I can say it was worth it, though I am not sure I would willingly accept it again. The capacity of my soul was expanded as I rediscovered these seven renewable energies of God. Yet what I went through was not a permanent fix. My mind still gets depleted, my spirit diminished and my capacity to love decreased. Our spiritual wind turbines have no way to store energy. We have only the promise that we will be given what we need, sufficient for the day.

My oldest son recently graduated from college. As I sat in the bleachers for the graduation ceremony the paradoxes of life transitions overwhelmed rather than energized me. I looked at the age lines on all the parents and wondered, *Why do they seem so old?* And then I looked in the mirror at my own age lines and sighed, *When did I get so old?* I was captivated by the youthful exuberance of the students, the endless possibilities ahead for them, their boundless horizon of time, even as I was imprisoned in my own thoughts by my time-bound, limited possibilities and exhausting life. I realized I was allowing comparison to twist my experience. Beyond that, I recognized in myself the telltale signals that I had reverted to my own energy rather than intentionally accessing God's energy. And so I was muddling through once again.

Two weeks later, as I was co-leading a retreat, we opened our time together by "laying the altar"—an intimate storytelling exercise. Each participant shared an image representing a pivotal moment or insight he or she had had since we were last together and then laid that image on the altar as their offering to the community. As I listened to their stories, it felt as if I was discovering the wellspring of God's energy once again.

They told stories of reclaimed identity (the energy of grace), renewed hope (the energy of possibility) and restored relationships after bitter conflict (the energy of paradox). As they were speaking, the energy behind their stories reinvigorated me and reconnected me, with them and through them, to the source of life present from the very creation of the world. "In the beginning . . . God created the heavens and the earth" (Gen 1:1). In that moment, God was re-creating my world . . . again.

Renewal: Not a One-Time Event

I share this story as a reminder that the life of faith is not "an every day and in every way I am getting better and better" enterprise. There are days when I am in the flow of God's creative, renewable energy, confident that I am a child of God, able to envision how I can uniquely serve and willing to extend myself sacrificially to the world. Other days I wonder and doubt and drag myself forward, assuming that the future of the world, my community and my family is all on my shoulders. Then I stagger under the unbearable weight of my attempts at self-sufficiency.

My story is my own, and I know that. But I sense it is also not a unique story. I am convinced most of us long for loving relationships and the energy to engage them fully. We yearn for meaningful work and the power to do it well. But whether we are able to do that in the long run depends on our energy source, our willingness to transfer from our own exhaustible energy to the renewable power of God's creative energies for our lives—not just once when we hit bottom and can do nothing else, but every day. Every hour. In every encounter: Being a loving parent when your child is in pain. Being a friend who will not give up on a friendship. Being a coworker who does his or her work honestly and encourages others. Having an eye for the outcast, a heart for those who suffer injustice and hands willing to sift through the muck of the world to reclaim those who have been muddied by it. These are the small works of God. They may be barely perceptible in the eyes of the world, but for those who receive them, at that moment, they mean the world.

Day by day, moment by moment, loving interaction by loving interaction, we learn to trust in the slow work of God. But, even more to the point, we learn to trust in the renewable energies of God that have been available from the very creation of the world, calming the waters of chaos, breathing life into dead bones, energizing surprisingly imperfect people for service and renewing my life and yours.

Receive them.

Embrace them

Trust them.

Live in them.

Acknowledgments

Life turns and turns and turns. Sometimes it feels as if we are chasing after the wind, fueled by our own diminishing energy, and wandering from task to task, from place to place, from relationship to relationship, all the while asking, *Is this all there is?* Other times it is as though we are a turbine standing tall in a wind farm catching the wind, being fueled by a power beyond our own, experiencing with gratitude and wonder *all there is!*

This book documents my movement from chasing the wind—a time in my life when I lived by my own power and initiative and suffered the consequences of an exhausted body, a depleted mind and a broken spirit—to catching the wind, a time in my life when I learned how to open myself to a power and energy not my own, an energy that was always present and always available to renew my body, my mind and my spirit.

Throughout my transition, I was gifted by many people who were experiencing similar life circumstances and who were willing to share their stories. I think I, like many of them, longed for the quick fix that would relieve my pain and renew the energy my life once had. But as opposed to ready-made solutions, I discovered the already-created wisdom embedded in God's story from the beginning.

I could not manufacture a more graceful attitude toward life, but I could open myself to the renewable energy of grace embedded in the creation story. Life comes to us as a daily gift from the Creator's hand (Gen 1:1).

I could not manufacture hope, but I could avail myself of the renewable energy of possibility embedded in the creation story. As God's Spirit once hovered over the waters of chaos (Gen 1:2), God's Spirit is still available, still present in the chaos of my life, energizing me with new possibility.

On and on, as I read through the creation story in Genesis 1:1–2:4, I was struck by its enduring wisdom and the life energy embedded within. Grace. Possibility. Paradox. The natural world. Relationships. Fruitful work. Rest. These energizing forces, which I so desperately needed in my life, were always present in God's life. And unlike nonrenewable sources of energy that we burn and lose, these energies are renewable from generation to generation, life to life, moment to moment.

My prayer is that you, the reader of this book, will linger over each chapter, ponder the questions, open yourself to the idea of each energy, consider how it can and does empower you and then trust God's slow, transformative work in your life.

The initial idea for this book was presented in my doctor of ministry thesis written to complete my degree at Fuller Seminary. I am grateful for the openness and encouragement of my advisors as this idea of the creative, renewable energies of God emerged.

During the process, there were many who added their own energy and insight. They became co-creators with me whether they were aware of their input or not. I am grateful for these energizing people.

For Patty, my wife, and for my children, Anders, Annika, Leif and Siri. In the process of singing and dancing, crying and laughing, failing and forgiving, you renew my life every day. I often shake my head in wonder and delight that we get to do this life together.

For family and friends who poured through portions of this book providing honest (sometimes brutally honest) feedback. You extended the renewable energy of relationship and possibility into my life with each encounter.

For the staff (past and present), leaders and members of Peace Lutheran Church in Gahanna, Ohio, who were, in many ways, my laboratory as I researched, developed and lived these ideas. I cannot thank you enough for your generosity of spirit and for giving me the time on sabbatical to bring these ideas to light.

For the Renovaré community. When we first met I was busy chasing after wind. Your friendship and wisdom encouraged me to begin catching the wind and gave me confidence that I had an important story to share.

For my new friends at IVP. For Bob Fryling, who saw something emerging in me that I only hoped would grow. For Cindy Bunch, who endured my barrage of novice questions with such grace.

Finally, for my mom and dad. Most of what I have written in this book you already had written into my life. Your personal stories inspire me. Your insightful and probing minds challenge me. Your generosity of time, energy and wisdom in this process humbled me. I only hope someday that others might experience the kind of deeply embodied, life-giving wisdom in my life that I experience in yours.

Study Guide

This study guide can be used individually or, preferably, in conversation with others. You could use it both to encourage an emerging friendship or deepen an existing relationship, one-on-one or in small groups. That being said, a few guidelines might be helpful.

First, listen to one another without judgment. The questions you will reflect on and the practices you will engage in are meant to deepen your connection with God, yourself, others and the natural world. The process may be joyful and energizing. There may also be times when it is painful or overwhelming. Whenever we probe deeper life realities, the potential exists to uncover parts of our lives and thinking that we would rather deny or hold within. Listening without judgment allows for the process of discovery and creates open space for God's Spirit to renew and re-energize.

Second, be consistent in meeting. Choose a time and space that will work regularly. Give each other enough time to read the material and do your own reflection prior to meeting. If you commit to a certain time frame (an hour or so), be diligent about keeping to the time frame, and pick up where you left off the next time you get together.

Third, be committed to the process. There are assigned practices for each chapter. Find the ones that are most needed in your life and the most potentially life giving for you. It is better to do a few things more intentionally than many things superficially. It may also be helpful to keep a journal of your personal reflections. Over time you will notice repeated themes and, hopefully, movements of growth.

Fourth, be graceful to one another. Sometimes life gets in the way, even when we have every good intention. How you treat one another is potentially a greater gift than what any reading and reflecting can offer. Respect each other's journey. Encourage each other. Enjoy life together.

There are five sections to each gathering time.

Check in. Use this time to catch up on life since you last met and also to ask about the practice each of you chose to do. How did it go? What was energizing about it? What kind of encouragement or support do you need to continue the practice?

Connect. Use the author's unfolding narrative to make connections to your personal narrative.

Contemplate. The questions are meant to help you dig deeper into the Essential Life Questions. If you end up focusing on just a few questions, no problem. This is not a test. Completing all the questions per session gains you no extra points. Pick up where you left off the next time you meet or choose to move on to another section.

Commit. The practices are designed to connect you with the renewing power of each of the energies. Again, it is better to practice a few things more intentionally than many things superficially. If you find one of the practices life giving, stay with it. You can always come back to the others later.

Close. There are multiple options for closing your time together: (1) Ask each other what one thing you will be working on leading up to the next gathering. Commit to pray for that one thing. (2) If comfortable, pray with each other, asking for specific issues you can hold up in prayer. (3) Simply say something like, "Thanks for being on the journey with me. See you next time." Choose what is best for you.

Introduction and Chapter 1:
The Renewable Energy of the Holy Spirit

Check in. If this is the first gathering, introduce yourself to each other and then respond to these questions: "What do I hope to gain from this experience?" and "What, if anything, makes me anxious about being in these kinds of conversations?"

Connect. What struck you about the author's opening stories? How do those stories connect with yours?

Contemplate.

- Which, if any, of the seven renewable, creative energies is most apparent in your life currently? Which do you long for? Why?

- Where do you see evidence of the three cultural distortions (pace of life, quick-fix mentality, seduction of more) in the world and in your life? What effect do they have on you?

- Think about a time when you were "muddling through." What was that experience like? What did you learn about yourself?

- Look at the "Is it possible" questions on page 31. In what area of your life is it easiest to acknowledge the Spirit's presence? Most difficult? Why?

Commit. Read through the practices at the end of the introduction and chapter one. Commit to trying one.

Close.

Chapter 2: The Energy of Grace

Check in. Describe your experience with the practice(s).

Connect. What struck you about the author's opening story? How does that story connect with yours?

Contemplate.

- Essential Life Question: What is my image of God?

    - What pictures (if any) of God did you have in your mind when you were growing up? What phrases would you use to describe God? Where do you think those pictures/phrases came from?

    - How has that image changed? What circumstances in your life caused you to re-examine your image of God?

    - If you were able to imagine a God of grace and love, how would that change how you see yourself, your life— imperfections and failures included?

- Essential Life Question: How does my image of God affect the way I see the world, others, my own life?

    - In what ways do you succumb to what the author calls "comparison fatigue?" What does that do to your sense of self? Can you think about and describe specific circumstances when you are more susceptible to the negative effects of comparison?

    - Reflecting on Laubach's phrase, "They must see God in me," how would you like others to see God's presence in you, in your life? If you feel bold enough, ask a friend or

family member to share how they see God's presence in
your life.

- Conversely, Laubach also asserts, "I must see God in
  them." What kinds of people do you have the hardest time
  seeing God's presence in? How could you learn more
  about "those people," whoever those people are for you?

Commit. Read through the practice. Commit to continuing
one of the practices or trying another.

Close.

Chapter 3: The Energy of Possibility

Check in. Describe your experience with the practice(s).

Connect. What struck you about the author's opening story?
How does that story connect with yours?

Contemplate.

- Essential Life Question: What hopes shape and give meaning
  to my life?
  - What gets you out of bed in the morning and gives you
    the energy you need for the day?
  - When in your life have you found yourself standing on
    one side of the "gap," hesitant to step across? What
    encouraged you to take the step? What kept you from
    taking the step?
  - Would you consider yourself a dreamer or a realist?
    What are the advantages or disadvantages of each?
  - How does St. Francis' phrase "Start by doing what's nec-
    essary; then do what's possible; and suddenly you are
    doing the impossible" connect with you? What steps
    does it encourage you to take as you move forward?

- Essential Life Question: What life resources give me the strength and courage to act?

  - When have you needed extra strength or courage in the past? Where has it come from? How would you connect God's energizing presence with that experience?

  - Imagine an upcoming day in your life. How would your interactions change if you engaged them with the young physician's guiding phrase, "integrity and intention?"

- Essential Life Question: What life practices might work for me?

  - When have you been frustrated by spiritual practices that seemed life renewing to others but left you depleted rather than energized?

  - Given who you are, not who you think you ought to be, what are some daily practices that may be energizing for you?

  - Rather than adding more to your life, can you reimagine some things you already do and use them as opportunities to be open to the energy of God's presence and possibility?

Commit. Read through the practices and commit to continuing one or trying another.

Close.

Chapter 4: The Energy of Paradox

Check in. Describe your experience with the practice(s).

Connect. What struck you about the author's opening story? How does that story connect with yours?

Contemplate.

- Essential Life Question: What life circumstances have forced me to wrestle with the paradox of light and darkness?

- Think about the image of an unwanted gift. What is helpful about that image as you consider the struggles you have had in life? What questions are left unanswered for you?

- Jacob's story in Genesis 32:22-32 reminds us that scars tell stories. Think about a scar that you have (physical, emotional, spiritual). What story does it tell?

- Essential Life Question: In what ways have I been blessed by an unwanted gift?

  - What have you learned about yourself, about God, because of an "unwanted gift?"

  - How do you deal with suffering that doesn't seem to have any answers?

- The author invites us to consider three responses to the paradox of light and darkness that we experience around us and within us: acceptance, resistance and presence. What was helpful for you in those responses? What questions do you still have?

Commit. Read through the practices and commit to continuing one or trying another.

Close.

Chapter 5: The Energy of the Natural World

Check in. Describe your experience with the practice(s).

Connect. What struck you about the author's opening story? How does that story connect with yours?

Contemplate.

- Essential Life Question: How can I allow the beauty of creation to inspire me?

- What parts of God's creation are most beautiful to you? How often do you get to see or experience them? What do they teach you about God? About yourself?

- The seasons of the natural world remind us of the hidden beauty in seasons of dormancy. What do those seasons teach us about our lives? About how God works?

- Seasons of growth and dormancy remind us of the spiritual gift of waiting. When, if ever, have you experienced waiting as a spiritual gift? What did you learn about yourself in those times?

• Essential Life Question: How can I honor my interconnectedness with the natural world through the choices I make each day?

- In a normal day, how often do you consider the connection between your actions (what you eat, what you spend, what you throw away, what you drive, etc.) and the natural world?

- What decisions will you continue to make to honor your connection with God's creation through the natural world?

- What decisions will you rethink because of the potential negative impact on the natural world?

Commit. Read through the practices and commit to continuing one or trying another.

Close.

Chapter 6: The Energy of Relationships

Check in. Describe your experience with the practice(s).

Connect. What struck you about the author's opening story? How does that story connect with yours?

Contemplate.

- Essential Life Question: How does affirming all people are created in the image of God affect how I see and treat them?

  - Do you ever think about yourself as created in the image of God? What thoughts or feelings does that conjure up within you?

  - Do you ever think about the people you interact with daily (at the store, at work, in your community, at home, on the street) as created in the image of God? Imagine what it might be like to do so. How would that change your interactions?

  - Relationships that change us are relationships that we "do deep." Describe one of those relationships you have had in your past or that you have currently. What makes the relationship so energizing for you?

- Essential Life Question: What keeps me from desiring, and therefore developing, deeper relationships?

  - The author addressed the issues of time and fear as impediments to deeper relationships. How have you experienced those impediments in your relationships? How have you chosen to overcome them?

  - Where have you experienced the "danger of a single story" in your own life? What have you done or could you imagine yourself doing to expand your soul by getting to know the story of a person of another culture, class, religion or race?

  - Reflect on the story that ended with the question, "Will you still be my friend if I never convert to Christianity?"

Are there deal breakers for you in relationships? If so, what are they?

- Do you think there are deal breakers for God in relationship with us? If so, what would they be?

- How do we reflect God's relationship with us through our relationship with others?

Commit. Read through the practices and commit to continuing one or trying another.

Close.

Chapter 7: The Energy of Fruitful Work

Check in. Describe your experience with the practice(s).

Connect. What struck you about the author's opening story? How does that story connect with yours?

Contemplate.

- Essential Life Question: What am I here for at this time?

  - Reflect on the story of the woman who discovered her calling as she volunteered in the adults with disabilities ministry. What are you doing now that fills you with a sense of deep satisfaction? What would you like to do but your fears or anxieties keep you from starting?

- Essential Life Question: What in my life brings me joy?

  - Make a list of those things that bring you joy. Which ones are you doing now? Celebrate them. Which ones would you like to be doing? How can you find the time or place to do them?

  - Reflect on the fruits of fruitful work (no distinctions, people over procedure, extra mile, humility). How are these fruits evident or absent in your workplace, the place you volunteer or your home? What can you do to manifest these fruits?

- Essential Life Question: What role does money—the accumulating of it and the spending of it—play in my sense of identity, my relationships, my use of time, my way of life?

  - What were the core messages you received about money when you were growing up? How are those messages helpful for you now? In what ways do you fight against them?

  - Why do you think Jesus taught so often about money and possessions? How do you connect the use of money with your life as a follower of Jesus?

  - What do you need to know more about in regard to a faithful use of your money and resources? Who can you consult?

  Commit. Read through the practices and commit to continuing one or trying another.

  Close.

Chapter 8: The Energy of Rest and Conclusion

Check in. Describe your experience with the practice(s).

Connect. What struck you about the author's opening story? How does that story connect with yours?

Contemplate.

- Essential Life Question: What does renewing rest look like for me?

  - Renewing rest takes different forms for each person. When have you experienced the renewing power of rest?

What did you notice about your body, your mind and your spirit following this time?

- Essential Life Question: What might I intentionally do to renew my body, my mind and my spirit?

  - A once-a-year vacation is not enough to renew our lives. Given your current life circumstances, what renewing, restful exercises can you put in place on a daily, weekly and seasonal basis?

  - In the conclusion, the author reminds us that renewal is a life-long process, not a one-time event. What have you learned about yourself that can be helpful when you enter another depleting cycle of life? What cues let you know that you are in need of renewal?

  - Now what? Essential life questions need to be considered and reconsidered at each new phase of life. Make a list of the Essential Life Questions that you need to spend more time reflecting on now. Find someone to take the journey with you.

Commit. Read through the practices and commit to continuing one or trying another.

Close.

Notes

Introduction: Energy Depletion

[1]"How the Last Decade Changed American Life," Barna.org, July 31, 2013, www.barna.org/barna-update/culture/624-how-the-last-decade-changed -american-life; quoting David Kinnaman.

[2]Jürgen Moltmann, *The Spirit of Life: A Universal Affirmation* (Minneapolis: Fortress, 1992), p. 86.

[3]Claus Westermann, *Genesis 1–11: A Continental Commentary* (Minneapolis: Fortress, 1994), p. 65.

[4]"How the Last Decade Changed American Life," www.barna.org/barna -update/culture/624-how-the-last-decade-changed-american-life.

[5]Ronald Heifetz, *Leadership Without Easy Answers* (Cambridge, MA: Harvard University Press, 1994), p. 22.

Chapter 2: The Energy of Grace

[1]Anne Lamott, *Traveling Mercies: Some Thoughts on Faith* (New York: Pantheon, 1999), p. 143.

[2]Frank C. Laubach, *Letters by a Modern Mystic* (Colorado Springs: Purposeful Design Publications, 2007), p. 12.

Chapter 3: The Energy of Possibility

[1]Bruce C. Birch, Walter Brueggemann, Terence E. Fretheim and David L. Peterson, *A Theological Introduction to the Old Testament* (Nashville: Abingdon, 1999), p. 48.

[2]Ian Morgan Cron, *Chasing Francis: A Pilgrim's Tale* (Colorado Springs: NavPress, 2006), p. 57.

[3]Ruth Richards, ed., *Everyday Creativity and New Views of Human Nature* (Washington DC: American Psychological Association, 2007), p. 39.

[4]Brad Hirschfield, *You Don't Have to Be Wrong for Me to Be Right: Finding Faith Without Fanaticism* (New York: Harmony, 2007), p. 241.

Chapter 4: The Energy of Paradox

[1]Claus Westermann, *Genesis 1–11: A Continental Commentary* (Minneapolis: Fortress, 1994), p. 114.

[2]Parker Palmer, *The Promise of Paradox: A Celebration of Contradictions in the Christian Life* (San Francisco: Jossey-Bass, 2008), p. xxi.

[3]Barbara Brown Taylor, *Learning to Walk in the Dark* (New York: HarperOne, 2014), p. 8.

[4]Ibid., p. 5.

[5]Walter Brueggemann, *Genesis*, Interpretation (Atlanta: John Knox Press, 1982), p. 268.

[6]Palmer, *Promise of Paradox*, p. 32.

Chapter 5: The Energy of the Natural World

[1]Brian McLaren, *A Generous Orthodoxy* (Grand Rapids: Zondervan, 2004), p. 242.

[2]Joseph Campbell and Bill Moyers, *The Power of Myth* (New York: Doubleday, 1988), p. 22.

[3]Daniel Goleman, *Focus: The Hidden Driver of Excellence* (New York: Harper-Collins, 2013), p. 139.

Chapter 6: The Energy of Relationships

[1]Claus Westermann, *Genesis 1–11: A Continental Commentary* (Minneapolis: Fortress, 1994), p. 158.

[2]Tom Rath, *Vital Friends* (New York: Gallup Press, 2006), p. 21.

[3]Daniel Goleman, *Social Intelligence: The New Science of Human Relationships* (New York: Bantam, 2006), p. 4.

[4]John Ortberg, *The Life You've Always Wanted* (Grand Rapids: Zondervan, 1997), p. 87.

Chapter 7: The Energy of Fruitful Work

[1]Claus Westermann, *Genesis 1–11: A Continental Commentary* (Minneapolis: Fortress, 1994), pp. 61-62.

[2]William L. Holladay, ed., *A Concise Hebrew and Aramaic Lexicon of the Old Testament* (Grand Rapids: Eerdmans, 1971), p. 261.

[3]Mihaly Csikszentmihalyi, *Flow: The Psychology of Optimal Experience* (New York: HarperCollins, 1990), p. 4.

[4]Jessica Lahey, "Why Kids Care More About Achievement Than Helping Others," *The Atlantic*, June 25, 2014, www.theatlantic.com/education/archive /2014/06/most-kids-believe-that-achievement-trumps-empathy/373378.

[5]Dallas Willard, *Hearing God: Developing a Conversational Relationship with God* (Downers Grove, IL: InterVarsity Press, 1999), p. 207.

Chapter 8: The Energy of Rest

[1]Claus Westermann, *Genesis 1–11: A Continental Commentary* (Minneapolis: Fortress, 1994), p. 172.

[2]Daniel Goleman, *Focus: The Hidden Driver of Excellence* (New York: Harper-Collins, 2013), p. 20.

[3]Richard J. Foster, *Prayer: Finding the Heart's True Home* (New York: Harper-Collins, 1992), p. 100.

[4]Ibid.

[5]Jürgen Moltmann, *The Spirit of Life: A Universal Affirmation* (Minneapolis: Fortress, 1992), p. 86.

About the Author

Kai Mark Nilsen (DMin, Fuller Seminary) has been lead pastor at Peace Lutheran in Gahanna, Ohio, for over ten years. He serves on the ministry team for Renovaré International, as faculty for the Renovaré Institute and as a certified pastoral coach for the Evangelical Lutheran Church in America. Nilsen is also a leader in the Gahanna Ministerial Association where he has collaborated with other community leaders to develop a cross-denominational community ministry.

Throughout his career, Nilsen's ministry has been motivated by a core conviction that God has planted in each of us the capability to love each other and the world, to serve those in need, to hope during dark times and to experience a full life in the present moment. He and his wife, Patty, have four children.

Connect with Kai on twitter (@kainilsen) or via email at renewyourlife17@gmail.com.

formatio

TRADITION. EXPERIENCE.
TRANSFORMATION.

Formatio books from InterVarsity Press follow the rich tradition of the church in the journey of spiritual formation. These books are not merely about being informed, but about being transformed by Christ and conformed to his image. Formatio stands in InterVarsity Press's evangelical publishing tradition by integrating God's Word with spiritual practice and by prompting readers to move from inward change to outward witness. InterVarsity Press uses the chambered nautilus for Formatio, a symbol of spiritual formation because of its continual spiral journey outward as it moves from its center. We believe that each of us is made with a deep desire to be in God's presence. Formatio books help us to fulfill our deepest desires and to become our true selves in light of God's grace.

What Is Renovaré?

Renovaré USA is a nonprofit Christian organization that models, resources, and advocates fullness of life with God experienced, by grace, through the spiritual practices of Jesus and of the historical Church. We imagine a world in which people's lives flourish as they increasingly become like Jesus.

Through personal relationships, conferences and retreats, written and web-based resources, church consultations, and other means, Renovaré USA pursues these core ideas:

- *Life with God* - The aim of God in history is the creation of an all-inclusive community of loving persons with God himself at the center of this community as its prime Sustainer and most glorious Inhabitant.

- *The Availability of God's Kingdom* - Salvation is life in the kingdom of God through Jesus Christ. We can experience genuine, substantive life in this kingdom, beginning now and continuing through all eternity.

- *The Necessity of Grace* - We are utterly dependent upon Jesus Christ, our ever-living Savior, Teacher, Lord, and Friend for genuine spiritual transformation.

- *The Means of Grace* - Amongst the variety of ways God has given for us to be open to his transforming grace, we recognize the crucial importance of intentional spiritual practices and disciplines (such as prayer, service, or fasting).

- *A Balanced Vision of Life in Christ* - We seek to embrace the abundant life of Jesus in all its fullness: contemplative, holiness, charismatic, social justice, evangelical, and incarnational.

- *A Practical Strategy for Spiritual Formation* - Spiritual friendship is an essential part of our growth in Christlikeness. We encourage the creation of Spiritual Formation Groups as a solid foundation for mutual support and nurture.

- *The Centrality of Scripture* - We immerse ourselves in the Bible: it is the great revelation of God's purposes in history, a sure guide for growth into Christlikeness, and an ever rich resource for our spiritual formation.

- *The Value of the Christian Tradition* - We are engaged in the historical "Great Conversation" on spiritual formation developed from Scripture by the Church's classical spiritual writings.

Christian in commitment, ecumenical in breadth, and international in scope, Renovaré USA helps us in becoming like Jesus. The Renovaré Covenant succinctly communicates our hope for all those who look to him for life:

> In utter dependence upon Jesus Christ as my ever-living
> Savior, Teacher, Lord, and Friend,
> I will seek continual renewal through:
> • spiritual exercises • spiritual gifts • acts of service

RENOVARÉ

Renovaré USA
8 Inverness Drive East, Suite 102 • Englewood, CO, 80112 USA • 303-792-0152
www.renovare.us